A Keeper of Bees

A Keeper of Bees

Notes on Hive and Home

ALLISON WALLACE

RANDOM HOUSE

NEW YORK

Copyright © 2006 by Allison Wallace

Published in the United States by Random House, an imprint of
The Random House Publishing Group, a division of
Random House, Inc., New York.

RANDOM HOUSE and colophon are registered
trademarks of Random House, Inc.

"The Work of Honeybees" was originally published in slightly
different form in the *Georgia Review*, Spring, 2003.

LIBRARY OF CONGRESS CATALOGING-IN-PUBLICATION DATA
Wallace, Allison.
A keeper of bees : notes on hive and home /
Allison Wallace.— 1st ed.
p.   cm.
Includes bibliographical references (p.).
ISBN 1-4000-6271-3
1. Wallace, Allison.   2. Beekeepers—Arkansas—Biography.
3. Honeybee—Arkansas—Anecdotes.   I. Title.
SF523.82.W35.A3 2006
638'.1—dc22
2005046688

Printed in the United States of America on acid-free paper

www.atrandom.com

2 4 6 8 9 7 5 3 1

FIRST EDITION

Book design by Dana Leigh Blanchette

For Blake

You'll begin to understand the life of bees once you're clear about the fact that the bee lives as if it were in an atmosphere pervaded thoroughly by love.

—RUDOLF STEINER,

Bees (translated from the German by Thomas Braatz)

Beekeeping is farming for intellectuals.

—SUE HUBBELL,

A Book of Bees

CONTENTS

Preface

"I think I could turn and live with animals," Walt Whitman wrote in "Song of Myself." "They are so placid and self-contain'd, / I stand and look at them long and long." He goes on:

> They do not sweat and whine about their condition,
> They do not lie awake in the dark and weep for their
>   sins,
> They do not make me sick discussing their duty to
>   God,
> Not one is dissatisfied, not one is demented with the
>   mania of owning things,
> Not one kneels to another, nor to his kind that lived
>   thousands of years ago,
> Not one is respectable or unhappy over the whole
>   earth.

Although most commentary focuses on the acerbic lines comparing animals to the poet's fellow Americans, Wendell Berry, one of my favorite authors, made me look twice at the opening line. "I think I could turn and live with animals" would have been written, Berry asserts, only by someone immersed in a culture generally unaware that "we *do* live with animals." Always have, and in some way or other always will. (For several intimate illustrations of this fact, see Roger M. Knutson's charming little books *Furtive Fauna* and *Fearsome Fauna,* subtitled as field guides to the creatures that live on us and within us.) Indeed, we don't merely live with animals, we live at all *because they live*—because they do the amazing, phenomenal things they do. Working in tandem with plants, animals give us by their very lives and deaths fertile soil, clean water, and clean air. And of course, they make it possible for us to eat, even those among us who do not eat any animals per se. This is especially true of honeybees, who pollinate not just the wildflowers gracing a spring meadow, but also many of the crops upon which we all depend.

Human beings have known the value of bees as an even more direct source of food—be it the honey they make or their own crunchy little bodies—for as long as they've been human. Yet none of these features drew me into the honeybees' world initially, although I've always enjoyed a bit of amber syrup on my toast and in my coffee, and although I was raised by a woman who swears by the consumption of locally produced honey to alleviate allergies to local pollens. No, my interest in bees took off when I discovered in one memorable season their own mixed nature: gentle, sun-dappled handmaidens to the hive in one moment, fierce little murderous crazies the next—though only if you get seriously in their way. The full story is told later in these pages, so for now I'll just say this was the summer I decided to live consciously with animals (besides my dog) for the rest of my days. From there it was a small step to another, closely related insight: that we don't just *live* with animals, we also *think* with them.* We humans have thought with honeybees for a very long time indeed: they have figured prominently in religious ideas and imagery (for example, the notion that honey is heaven-sent—literally, that it falls to earth from above—shows up in many ancient, polytheistic belief systems, lending it a sacred quality); in fables and folklore (such as the old European insistence that news of a beekeeper's death must be broken gently to the bees themselves, else they, too, will perish); and in symbols of and metaphors for concepts like hard work, cooperation, thrift, purity, even political economy.

Sometimes the honeybee leads my own thoughts down such well-worn paths, but now and again she catches and follows the trail of scents coming from other, less heavily traveled directions, and I stay on her heels (that is, I would if she had any). Together we go traipsing, for instance, after the kinetic, ever-changing nature of biological creation and re-creation, in which every living being participates, consciously or otherwise. Or we attend awhile to the enduring appeal (to both of us) of moving on to new scenes when the old ones seem to have lost their power to answer some deep-seated, inexpressible yearning. Then, too, there's the tension that arises when the opposite of this urge to move on kicks in: here I mean the urge to stay still, to put down a long taproot, to say with the conviction of a Mor-

---

*Ecological philosopher Paul Shepard is particularly valuable to read on this point.

mon that *this is the place*. And finally, my honeybee and I go nosing after the most compelling question I know to ask—explored far more ably by philosophers and theologians than I could ever manage—the question whether anything in the physical world can ever reveal metaphysical truth.

While following the bee down these twisting lanes, I'm also trying to keep a steady eye on the creature herself. A child asked Whitman, "What is the grass?" and the poet responded that he did not know. Neither do I know what exactly is *Apis mellifera*, or honey, or wax, or the flowers or rain or sun or soil that, together, make all the rest happen. But I do know there are worse ways to squander one's time than trying to find out. Until that happy day of revelation arrives, I content myself with the hive as a transporting vision of the simplest perfection that seems possible on this earth: glowing gold and bronze, its many adepts unselfconsciously engaged in creative, productive work, their remarkable wax combs blessed with plenty and holding out the promise of more to come.

If you who read this would don the nylon veil—would take up beekeeping—understand right now that this isn't your how-to book, though you'll certainly need one of those. (Make that a half dozen.) This is by turns a how-not-to book, and a how-is-*that*-possible? book, the musings not of an expert but of a bumbling lover, whose contemplative disposition is frequently at odds with her desire to achieve a decent honey harvest. This is a modest record of things sought after more often than found, of things longed for more often than obtained. Notions hinted at, in other words, by glimpses we all get now and then of a restive, tireless, blossom-probing, black-and-topaz honeybee.

To those who helped along the way I owe a great many thanks, starting with Jamey Tippens and Nettie Lassiter, for turning my head with one small hive, and for offering friendship and support across years of changing circumstances. Tom Stumpf—book conversationalist par excellence—introduced me to Virgil and his bees, and to other wonderful classical and neoclassical writers besides. Doug Fox, David Doussourd, Stella Capek, Linda Hasselstrom, Norb Schedler, John Parrack, William Rossi, and Doug Corbitt all assisted in their various ways with the research that went into these chapters. I am indebted to Rick Scott and the University of Central Arkansas for freeing me up periodically from teaching to write. Rick also read and critiqued portions of the manuscript, as did Lisa Carl and T. R. Hummer. The indefatigable Rebecca Barnhouse read all of it thoughtfully, and passed along many wonderful honeybee-themed news articles and lines of medieval poetry; her encouragement, wry wit, and friendship over the years have made more difference than I can say, and not just to my writing. Several friends and colleagues with the Association for the Study of Literature and Environment (ASLE) provided terrific encouragement, too, not least among them Cheryll Glotfelty, Mike Branch, and Sydney Landon Plum. Many college students I've been honored to know were also helpful, if indirectly—even the one whose arrogant pronouncement "I feel no need to play fair with nature" shocked me into thinking hard about why we all should.

My agent, Wendy Strothman, and my editor, Susanna Porter, were invaluable critics, advisers, and finally midwives of the project. And my mother, Lynn Lupo, believed in this endeavor and in me all along, because she foolishly and sweetly believes I can do anything.

A Keeper of Bees

1

The Work of Honeybees

Even the insects in my path are not loafers, but have
their special errands. Not merely and vaguely in this
world, but in this hour, each is about its business.
—HENRY DAVID THOREAU,
Journal, September 30, 1852

It is measured in droplets, flakes, grains. All natural materials, some produced by their own bodies. The work of
bees aims at mass, strength, durability, longevity, achieving
these with particles that, taken alone, would blow away in
the slightest breeze. The work of bees appears in constant
need of doing, though once they've established a solidly respectable colonial home, it's hard to see why. I peer into
one of my hives—a marvelous multichambered palace
weighing a hundred pounds in wax, honey, pollen, and
stored brood—and say aloud, "Look, gang, time to kick
back and take it easy for a bit, don't you think? Haven't
you earned a break?" But no: they're as hard at it as ever,
every one of these thousands of murmuring engines roaming across the comb on her particular mission of the mo-

ment. And if ever this hive begins to feel too small, if the volume of the bees' work begins to push uncomfortably at the sturdy pine walls and inner cover, about half of them will take to the sky in search of nature's vacant lots for sale or rent, some hollow in a tree or rock overhang where a new colony can be established. The work of bees can slow down, can pause (during a northern winter, for example), but it can never really cease. And though most of us don't know it, we have reason to be deeply grateful this is so.

Every morning for a whole school year, the same thin-shouldered college boy could be found swabbing the tiled stairway separating me from my office when I arrived for work. Generally embarrassed at the sight of people doing any kind of cleaning on my behalf, I would tiptoe self-consciously onto the damp tile, apologize ("Sure, no prob"), and occasionally try to offer some variation on your basic "Nice work." By degrees I came to realize that he worked some afternoon shifts, too, when once again he plied his mop over every step, perhaps ticking them off one, two, three in his head as he slicked them. Ignorant of the young man's name, I was free to think of him as Sisyphus. He may have been fortunate in having only to drag a mop down the stairs rather than push a rock up a mountain, but there still remained for him the daily problem of ruined work in need of doing all over again. No matter that he'd left the tile a shiny chocolate brown before heading to class the day before: every morning and many afternoons there they'd be, a set of stairs newly begritted and grimed.

As I say, I was myself arriving for work each morning that I encountered this fellow. And how many student essays had I already marked in my time, how many classes taught, meetings attended, sloppy committee reports mopped up? It did not much matter, since there was always another one waiting—and by some grace or other I never thought to drive myself daft ticking them off one at a time.

Such appears to be the futile nature of most work: for every floor scrubbed, shirt sewn, wall painted, brick laid, wire strung, bale tossed, net hauled, baby delivered, engine tuned, meal prepared, report written, form processed, purchase order filled, confession heard, steer branded, or broken bone set, another just behind awaits its turn. The fact may be the sweetest dream that labor knows (as Frost put it), but let's not be fooled: each fact achieved by work *is* nevertheless a dream, a dissolution in the making, a ruin waiting to unfold. There is no such thing as work done that *stays* done: even God—or, if you prefer, organic evolution—seems not to have called it a day (not on the seventh, not on the six million and seventh), called it good, and given up tinkering. For mere mortals, the impermanence of achievement is an old, familiar source of grief. Listen to the Preacher:

> Then I looked on all the works that my hands had
>   wrought,
> And on the labor that I had labored to do,
> And, behold, all was vanity and vexation of spirit,
> And there was no profit under the sun.

Fast-forward a few hundred years nearer our own time, and here comes the thin, robed figure of Gandhi stepping up to say, maddeningly, that although everything I do will be insignificant, I must do it anyway. Stopping short, I peer into the apparition of his raisin-brown face: *But why?*

Animals generally and insects in particular appear not the least afflicted by such questions, though their work, too, is consistently undone by the same law of entropy that has set its face against permanent human achievement. Those bees of mine, for example, and their exquisitely built environment inside the hive: they tend it endlessly because it is endlessly subject to the vicissitudes of temperature, humidity, and the differential pressure exerted by thousands of tiny, hairy honeybee feet. To leave off housekeeping for even a day would be to court disaster, since the hive (especially in summer) is a very active nursery, where the near constant birthing of bee babies makes for a constant mess in need of tidying up.

The great majority of honeybees in a given colony are infertile females, and there's a reason they're called worker bees; there's reason in the phrase "busy as a bee." While the males or drones have their one job, that of mating with queens from other colonies (outside the hive, high up in the air), and while the queen has her one job of laying eggs (as many as two thousand on a really good summer's day), each worker bee has nearly a dozen jobs. Certain tasks are usually taken up as she reaches a certain age, and she usually takes them up in roughly the sequence followed by her sisters, though the overall condition of the colony can affect these patterns somewhat: the colony's needs always take precedence over any one worker bee's "need" to fulfill a given role. Like human children in a well-ordered home, the workers have their various chores, all assigned according to the bees' ages and abilities, or more precisely, their degree of physiological development. But unlike children's growth, honeybee development appears to speed up or slow down as the colony's well-being demands. Imagine being able, at will, to turn your toddlers into teenagers overnight, just because the housework has come to include some heavy lifting.

Suppose it's high summer. In some nondescript region of honeycomb in one of my hives, a newly matured worker bee is chewing and pawing her way out of the wax cell in which she has been nestled, growing, for a couple of weeks. In order to keep up with her in the throng of bees she's about to join, let's daub a bit of fluorescent orange paint on her back, and for ease of reference, let's call her Bella. When she is finally freed from her chamber, the first thing she does is turn around and clean it of any debris she may have left behind, like a newborn tidying up its own afterbirth. She soon moves on to do the same for other brood (larval) cells, joining thousands of newborns who are similarly occupied, many of whom will poke around in Bella's cell, too, to be sure it's clean. (Honeybees are nothing if not thorough.) Bella and her young sisters may keep this up for only a day, or for as long as thirty days in rare instances. During this time, many will also begin capping brood or nursery cells—that is, sealing off with a wax cap the larvae that are ready to pupate. The wax has come afresh from the bees' own bodies, one flake at a time emerging from the upper abdomen like paper from a fax machine, in response to glandular signals. Or it could be that some of the caps are recent castoffs from newly emptied cells; recycling of this sort saves precious energy.

Before long Bella's body has responded to further physiological prompting and has begun to produce "brood food," a glandular secretion mixed with a bit of honey, water, and digestive enzymes. (As larvae age, until their cells are capped for pupation, they will also be fed some pollen, important to them for its protein.) This brood food Bella will dole out in tiny, one-droplet doses at the inner edges of larval cells, each time she pokes her head into one and determines the larva therein is deservingly hungry. By no means does she often reach that conclusion: she's at once a fussy and a stingy nanny, unable to refrain from constantly looking in on the babes yet rarely willing to dispense a warm bottle. Which is just as well, since, again, Bella is one of thousands making the nursery rounds at all hours: honeybee young are among nature's most doted upon.

Days pass. Having reared her share of brats in her time, Bella's about ready to move up into royal service—tending the queen. The lady of the hive must be frequently stroked, petted, and generously fed mouth-to-mouth helpings of brood food. She must also have her chamber pot emptied— that is, her feces carried away. Her every need anticipated by Bella and a half dozen or more daughters who keep close beside her, she moves steadily all the while over the brood comb, looking for clean, empty beds in the nursery to fill with more eggs. (And though Her Majesty seems to reign over the scene, let her fail regularly in this, her one grave duty, and the otherwise servile worker bees will forthwith have off with her head, trotting in a replacement queen raised by themselves.) Now Bella is more heavily drenched than usual in the queen's perfume—her special pheromone. This substance she and the other royal attendants will unwittingly spread out among the rest of the colony, giving all the bees there a sense of family identity. They may *look* like any other honeybees on the block, but they won't *smell* like them.

Bella may now be ten or twenty or perhaps even thirty days old. She's cleaning the hive of debris, such as dead bees, of which there are always some; the queen's egg laying occurs as steadily as it does precisely because there's always a certain amount of dying going on here, as each bee's life runs its course. Bella is also building comb—again, with wax she's produced herself—forming near-perfect hexagonal cells, each of which shares its walls with adjacent hexagons in a geometric miracle that maximizes space and architectural strength as circles or squares could not. And she's helping to process the nectar and pollen that are coming into the hive via the foraging bees. The pollen storage is begun by the foragers themselves, who scrape it off their back legs where they had stored it temporarily, during flight, in the middle of some hairs that curl around to form a kind of basket. Look—there's one scraping herself clean now. And here comes Bella, the bee with the orange spot on her back. Her newest job is to moisten the pollen pellets with saliva and regurgitated honey and to pack them into solid plugs securely within their cells. As for the nectar also arriving daily—the sweet, watery secretions collected by bees from blooming flowers of all kinds—that, too, is Bella's responsibility now, whenever a returning forager gets her attention. Taking the nectar into her mouth from the regurgitating bee, she spends a few minutes opening and closing her mouth around it (presumably to begin the evaporation process), then tucks it into a cell well above the brood nest, where it will undergo further evaporation before being sealed off, later on, with a wax cap. To aid in this all-important evaporation period (nectar must lose 82 percent of its water content to become honey), Bella and thousands of sisters fan their wings over the cells here at the top of the hive; at other times, they do the same down below, at the hive entrance, helping in the process to air-condition the whole building.

A few more days pass. Soon Bella is at the entrance regularly, getting a glimpse of the wide world while she now does sentry duty: each bee alighting at the entrance and seeking admission had better have about her a whiff of *this* hive's pheromone, or Bella will turn bouncer.

Having reached her prime in as few as a dozen and as many as forty to sixty days of age, Bella gets ready to fly. The glands that had produced wax and brood food now atrophy. In her first attempts—very short "orientation flights" only, to be sure she has landmarks by which to find the hive again later—Bella's brain actually undergoes subtle changes, and at this time (oh, finally!) she gets to expel her own feces, something she hasn't been willing to do indoors. (Elimination just makes more work for everybody, and who needs that?) Flying and foraging for water, nectar, pollen, and propolis—plant resins that bees use as "glue" within the hive; making dozens of trips daily between the hive and the surrounding fields and woods: all this will take every mite of energy she can summon over the next several days. And then it will kill her, essentially by wearing her out. Here lies Bella the bee, a hard worker gone to a deserved rest.

At the risk of stating the obvious, one might observe that work is not generally easy: we derive the word "labor" from the Latin verb *labi,* to slip or fail, to stagger under a weight. Sisyphus growing ever more fatigued with each upward shove of the rock; Bella wearing her wings and her life away fighting the wind that would bar her way back to the hive. The same Latin root gives us "lapse." Not for nothing is it said, then, that after their great lapse, Adam and Eve were made to labor for the rest of their days. If we may compare small things with great, Bella and all her laboring kin are in estimable company.

Yet she did get quite a lot of rest during her short summer weeks of life—prior to flying, anyway. Perhaps the honeybee's best-kept secret is that, though she appears to work like the dickens around the clock, she actually does a good deal of strolling or loitering on comb corners during part of every hour. How can this be, you ask, since so much astonishing work really does get done—many hundreds of wax cells built, many thousands of larvae reared, many pounds of honey put up in storage, one drop at a time? It would appear, as the old saw tells us, that many hands (or feet) do indeed make light work: with up to eighty thousand bees looking after business in a strong colony at the height of summer, the real wonder is that they don't make a mess of the job, getting in one another's way.

Bella's wintertime sisters get even more rest, since numerous tasks, especially foraging tasks, aren't begging for attention at that time of year. Most of these girls' work consists in keeping one another and the precious queen warm, not by hibernating, as many believe, but by drawing tightly together into a ball with the queen near the center, and keeping the ball in slow, constant motion all winter long— the toasty bees on the inside gradually crawling to the outside to take the places of the chilled ones, who in turn move in for a brief stay near the colony's inner fire. The extra rest these winter workers get appears to mean longer life, as many as three or four months longer than the summer bees'. Even so, a single worker bee, no matter what time of year she's born, doesn't live to celebrate a birthday.

For all the work performed in a normal hive throughout most weeks of the year, the rub still is—you guessed it—the fact that every bit of it has to be done countless times over. Every task completed will have to be taken up anew, if not by this worker bee then by that one, if not this summer season then the next. *Everything you do will be insignificant, but you must do it anyway.* The question persists: What in the world *for*?

For the sake of the world itself, it seems, for starters. For the very *formation* of the world. Scott Russell Sanders writes of the "force of spirit" in a recent book by that title, but I find myself dwelling on the force of form—on the force with which spirit demands manifestation. The unspeakably powerful spirit of biological life comes we know not whence and goes we know not where, but it always does so in *forms*—a wax cell here, a beaver lodge there; an orchard heavy with fruit, a stream dammed into habitat for water striders and wading birds. A world built and re-built, world without end, so long as bees and beavers go about their work. Things do not fall altogether apart—at least, not right away, and not until some other creature comes along, say a bacterium of some kind, whose own special work it is to dismantle the world. And even then, the scattering of molecules out there in the fallen leaves is prelude to some new construction project or other. The center does hold for a while, as long as every being at the periphery keeps to its given work, its given activity, its own in-form-ation.

That is, while at work a creature is not just shaping its own little corner of the world: it is also forming itself, coming into its own (we might say), living out its own form's dictates. In his wonderful little book *The Hungry Soul,* Leon Kass writes that "to be something, to be a particular animal in the full sense, is to be that animal-at-work: Really to be a squirrel means to be actively engaged in the constellation of activities we can call 'squirreling.' " "Do your work," wrote Emerson in a similar vein, "and I shall know you. Do your work, and you shall reinforce yourself." For us as for animals, the work we undertake is a major key to our identity: if we're lucky, we do work that we have been formed for. (If only each of us could know what that is, as easily as a squirrel or a honeybee knows!) It seems that a big reason we work is just to realize something of who we are—to find out what we're made of, what we're capable of. Be we tinker, tailor, soldier, or spy, we yearn to find out which of the world's countless itches we were born to scratch.

For work can be performed only upon the world, in response to problems (using the word loosely here) presented by other forms, by phenomena lying outside ourselves. Just as the eye sees only when it encounters an object to be seen, just as the tongue tastes only in the presence of flavor, so the elements of identity—will, energy, brain, opposable thumbs in a person, compound eyes in a honeybee—join forces and go to work only when some part of the world presents itself in invitation. A flower oozes sweet, minute droplets of nectar; another flower sheds its golden dust, a little of which the visiting bee will accidentally deposit on the next flower over, nestled in a branch just inches away, in the course of her work. And all so that spirit may soon say, *Peach. Orange. Almond. Pecan.* Behold, all work is vanity and vexation of spirit—but first it is beauty, in-form-ation, spirit's good news. Creation itself, shining wet and new as youth and maiden on that first day of their perfect, prelapsarian beginning.

"The forms of beauty fall naturally around the path of him who is in the performance of his proper work; as the curled shavings drop from the plane, and borings cluster around the auger," wrote Thoreau. Thus will the neighborhood of honeybees grow fatly into an orchard, and the orchard will nourish children and squirrels and juncos and mushrooms and earthworms and springtails. And these in their turn will do unto the world as it has done unto them, for good and for ill, and always in spirit's fantastic guises.

2

The Bees of My Youth*

I will arise and go now, and go to Innisfree,
And a small cabin build there, of clay and wattles
    made;
Nine bean rows will I have there, a hive for the
    honey bee,
And live alone in the bee-loud glade.

                    —W. B. YEATS,
              "The Lake Isle of Innisfree"

I.

Who can say what a beginning is, much less when? All stories begin in medias res. So if I tell you I began keeping bees
one spring some dozen years ago, picture me in my late
twenties, a couple of years married, happily puttering
about in a sunny woodland clearing in central North Carolina, planning a garden. The world all around is ancient,
its rocks and dirt, bugs, birds, and greenery having been

*With apologies to Jo Ann Beard, author of *The Boys of My Youth*.

shaped in the direction of this day for millennia. But it's a young world, too: this is only April of the year, with so many sweet things unfolding in perfect form and bright as morning. Just out of reach in the boughs fringing this space, little twiggy nests are taking the shape of cradles, and all around the air is abuzz with world-making business.

Here I began keeping bees by keeping, more or less successfully, out of their way. But before I can fully tell that story, I have to say why "here" mattered so—how it prepared me to think seriously about bees, among so many other things.

We had answered an ad in the paper for a cabin available for rent in the country, though he wasn't nearly as keen as I was on moving out so far. Impoverished graduate students and part-time teachers that we were, he thought we might just as well stay in our ratty little brick duplex near the university, rather than take on the expense and hassle of commuting fifteen curvaceous and partially unpaved miles in our big boat of a '77 Plymouth. But I had wearied of the noisy, shabby neighborhood that was all we could afford in town, where the soft Southern air was regularly assaulted by bad mufflers and student stereos booming along on big wheels spitting asphalt crumbs, and where the grass, the shrubs, the trees, and even the birds all seemed dusty, tattered, and tired. I wanted to walk out of the house with my dog and not feel immediately worried for him in traffic; I wanted to spy on birds from my front stoop with binoculars and not be taken for a busybody spying into people's windows. I wanted to plant lettuces, peas, potatoes, beans, sweet corn. Basil, oregano, tomatoes (six varieties), strawberries, cantaloupes. Blueberries, almonds, peach and apple orchards.

Calling the number in the paper, I was given complicated directions to the place—this was going to be a hideaway cabin for sure, requiring a dozen trips just to memorize the route. Eventually Mark and I would make hundreds of drives out to the home that came, for three years, to hold our happiest days together. Built from the logs of an old tobacco barn, the ashy-gray kind that's slowly sinking all over Carolina into clay and kudzu, the cabin had a central room with a woodstove where a tall, three-paneled, south-facing window made up one side, and a kitchen sink, stove, and old fridge made up the other; two small flanking rooms with lofts; a tiny room with a tub and shower; a tin roof; and, attached to one outer wall of the structure, a composting privy. Located one long stone's throw away (supposing you could have managed not to hit a tree) from the cabin in which our landlords resided, the place squatted comfortably in the vicinity of two hand-built tool sheds, several piles of lumber—our builder-landlord's wealth could be read in his many, careful piles—and an active chicken coop. A couple hundred acres of woods. A quarter mile of gravel driveway (ELVIS PRESLEY BLVD. read the green-and-white sign nailed to a tree) separating both homes from the main road. And room—about forty yards down a winding, shady path from our cabin to the much sunnier strip of land kept free of trees by the power company—for a garden.

The patch of ground Jamey and Nettie allotted me

wasn't much more than that, a patch. Naturally they kept for themselves the majority of the garden space in that little clearing, since they'd been working it for nearly twenty years. Along the western edge, its back to the woods, stood a beehive, one of those standard, silver-topped, two-story white boxes you occasionally see in a country field. Its front opening faced the square of ground I'd been granted—to torment me, I came to believe, though much later I understood the hive had been placed, some years before, to catch the first rays of the sunrise.

This was to be my first real garden, so I had plans enough to fill a couple of acres, much less the eight or ten square feet that, until I arrived, had been "approach" territory for Jamey's honeybees. Even before Mark and I had fully completed our move, I got to work turning the soil and preparing tightly ordered beds; it soon became evident that someone forgot to tell the bees they'd have company this year out in that slim, sunlit space where the power cut bisected the woods. The fact dawned on them, and they promptly let me know how they felt about it.

Zzzip! A furious, noisy tussle within my hair, like someone trapped in a nightmare of bedsheets, then a sudden quiet pause. *Yeow!* Nailed in the top of the head. A bee's response to any perceived assault is to sting the offender, and since hair can't be stung, this one went for the next best thing. A few days later it was déjà vu all over again, right in the seat of my baggy jeans. Ta-da, surprise. But no surprise, really, considering I had backed up to the hive while digging around, unaware in my green-bean daydream how close I was getting to its wooden bottom lip.

This served as a takeoff and landing board for bees coming and going on their foraging flights, and since they were flying more by instruments than by direct sight (stay tuned for details), the looming wall of my jeans didn't figure in their calculations. And a bee's response to any perceived assault—well, like I said.

Okay, now they had my attention. I knew vaguely that honeybees leave you alone if you leave them alone, and although I thought I *was* leaving them alone ("Just let me get the broccoli in, will you, girls?"), we suffered a difference of opinion. *I* suffered; they died, one at a time, with each sting. Determined to ease our conflict by giving them a wider berth, I concentrated for a while on planting other parts of my patch, leaving the young broccoli plants to fend for themselves.

What was it like, what was it all about. Many intervening years of change—a dissertation finally written; a move to Maine and another, much later, to Arkansas, following teaching jobs; the move of a husband out of my life—may bathe that first season of country living with lemony memory light, too lovely to trust. But what do you say we take our chances. The first thing I heard each morning as I headed down the footpath to the garden, warm coffee mug in hand, was the quiet. No traffic, no stereos or TVs. A thin breeze tossing the tops of the pines high overhead. (Oh. *That's* why all the cut-over subdivisions are called Whispering Pines.) A woodpecker making his rounds, the pitch of his hammering shifting slightly with each new tree. Lisping chickadees, towhees scratching in last fall's leaves and needles, mockingbirds gleefully mocking other birds.

Squirrels squirreling. The wordless flit and drift of pale blue butterflies in the warming sun. My little rusty-brown mutt rubbing one ear with a paw, dropping and rolling sensuously in the dirt, then standing up to turn around twice and settle himself in a drift of crispy leaves he'd found in the shade. The rhythmic scrape and slice of my shovel as I worked my way down one side of the garden, turning that orangy-yellow clay that passed for soil, watching it shear away from the blade in slabs the texture of hard ice cream. (With one such downward shove and upward thrust, I was horrified to find I'd sliced a live frog in half, just behind the shoulders. Its bulging eyes and wide, gasping mouth turned up toward me, as if pleading for an explanation.) Nearby, a bee going full throttle as it lifted off from one peach blossom, suddenly killing its engines to plop softly onto another. And, later in the season, cicadas tuning up their piercing whine, the sound that means high summer in Carolina.

Not that this paradise was without its serpents. Real ones, to begin with, serious customers like copperheads. But most were harmless garter and king snakes and all were turgid sleepyheads until the spring mornings began to lose their cool. Deer ticks caught a ride in the hair of your arms as you passed near the trees; chiggers insinuated their mean, itty-bitty selves between your skin and the waistband of your underwear. Mosquitoes hovered with dainty menace in your ears and just beyond your eyes. And those lovely, diaphanous blue butterflies? Agents of destruction, laying eggs on succulent garden seedlings so the caterpillars to come wouldn't have far to go for groceries.

Which meant the broccoli would need tending, after all, with an occasional dusting of Bt—a powder Jamey told me about that carried billions of naturally occurring bacteria (*Bacillus thuringiensis*) lethal to caterpillars but harmless to everything else. Thanking him for the tip, I ventured to mention the location of the crop in question: Beehive Central.

I was still very much at the beginning of what turned out to be a rather long journey, that of Learning to Read Jamey. His fleeting glance toward the hive from where we stood at his end of the garden told me he'd heard what I'd said; the quick return of his glance to the chickweed he was uprooting with a shovel, along with a soft "Hmm," told me he'd prefer not to think about or discuss it quite yet, or perhaps ever.

All too soon spring gave way to the thick, humid folds of summer, when each day seemed to sink in heavy, wet woolen layers over your head and shoulders. Some days it was exercise enough just to sit in a simple wooden chair and sweat. The swelter that had, by June, moved in for a long stay did no more for the bees' mood than it did for mine. They still took off from the hive in eager squadrons each morning, but by noon thick clumps of them hung about the hive's bottom entrance like bored bums around a pool hall. Eventually I would learn to see in this behavior a sign of great changes to come, but for now I just saw panting, irritable, would-be bullies spoiling for a fight. I maintained a careful distance, thankful the broccoli plants were now big enough to crouch behind.

Our cabin had no air conditioning, and though there

were screened doors and windows we could open, that
didn't mean much, what with no breeze and humidity
enough to dampen towels. Even taking off all your clothes
couldn't bring relief. But hiking nearly a mile of thickly
wooded trails to a nearby pond and *then* stripping everything off—well, that was worth a try once in a while.
Sometimes Mark joined me; always the Ben-dog trotted
happily along, in love with the coming and going (so many
flowers and weeds to sniff, so little time!) but decidedly
loath to pass beyond the pond's sandy shore. Just as well:
anyone taking a dip there had to share the water with the
countless toe- and elbow-nibbling bream with which the
pond had been stocked. Better to keep your bath brief and
emerge refreshed, ready to take up the fishing pole you'd
brought along so as to exact a little satisfying revenge.
Only two or three of those outings yielded fish big enough
to trouble with cleaning and frying, and even then they
were too bony to enjoy eating. Most of what I caught
either went back into the pond alive or else served to fertil-
ize my compost pile. The afternoon sun finally relenting by
about six o'clock, we'd commence a slow, thoughtful walk
back home, stopping on the way at an old, abandoned garden in a clearing to search out any fresh spears of asparagus that had outlived the gardener's neglect. Now the
woodland trails were free of the cobwebs we'd had to
break through on our trek to the pond, and deep carpets
of pine needles exhaled a warm, fragrant, end-of-the-day
sigh.

It may have been July, if memory serves, before my
complaints convinced Jamey that moving his beehive

would likely be in everyone's best interests—we'd all enjoy a little peace for a change, him included. In classic Jamey Tippens fashion, he thought it all out ahead of time but kept his deliberations to himself, until one moonless evening when the four of us, Jamey and Nettie, Mark and I, were out walking together along a nearby gravel road. "It's dark enough, we could move that colony tonight." I glanced up at him to make sure I'd heard right, as he went on to say that bees are afraid of the dark and would therefore likely stay put in their box when they felt it in motion. No need, he thought, either to wear protective clothing or to seal the bees up inside while we took them on this very short trip. As usual Mark was quick to say he'd be happy to help, but I kept to myself a little thrill of anxiety. I'd long assumed that if and when the hive ever got moved, strong and independent Jamey would do it himself. Nettie's flashlight beam played across the white gravel under our feet as we crunched along. Bypassing the short footpath through some trees that would have taken us to our respective cabins, we followed the road around a bend to where our garden—and the beehive—lay off to one side, just beyond a narrow strip of pines, in the power cut.

We stepped carefully in the dark direction of the hive. I was surprised to see that Jamey had already wheeled out to it a small, rusty child's wagon, the one he and Nettie sometimes used around the place for hauling things like bags of autumn leaves. Mark and I stood there, dubious communicants at an erstwhile untouchable altar, while Jamey laid out the plan. Crouching on either side, he and Mark would lift all at once the whole two-story outfit off its makeshift

cinder-block stand, about knee high. I would push the little wagon into place underneath, and Nettie would keep
the flashlight trained on the wagon so the guys could see
where to ease the hive down till it balanced along the metal
rim. Jamey would then take charge of the wagon handle
and begin pulling slowly, while the rest of us kept a hand
on the boxes to prevent excessive rocking as everything
went into motion.

Jamey explained that we weren't going far the first night:
to relocate a hive a short distance away without compro-
mising the colony's well-being, you can move it only about
ten or twelve inches a day in the chosen direction. This is
because the field force—those thousands of honeybees em-
ployed on any given day in gathering water, nectar, and
pollen from the surrounding woods and meadows—leave
the hive each morning with an exact sense of how to find it
upon their return. Move their front door more than a foot,
and they won't be able to locate it again. They'll fumble
about in the grass where their home used to be, and within
a day or two they'll die there. This is extraordinary, when
you think about it—here they've got these huge compound
eyes, with which they can find their way back to the very
spot they left hours ago, despite having traveled a circuit of
some two or three miles or even double that, yet a hive re-
located just a few too many inches to one side of its original footprint might as well be in Timbuktu for all it means
to them. Meanwhile, the house bees—and the brood
they're tending—will begin to suffer for lack of the supplies the field bees have not been able to bring them. In

other words: move a hive too far at one time, and the entire colony will begin to die. But field bees returning to a hive that's been only a little displaced will bump into its right-hand edge, say, where they expected to find the left edge; these bees will manage okay. They'll find their way to the entrance, unload their goods, and before departing again they'll reorient themselves, using the sun's location in the sky relative to their own near the ground, and maybe a local landmark or two as well, to the new site so as not to be fooled again upon a future return. Except that, if a beekeeper is trying to move a colony farther across his beeyard, then those field bees will indeed be fooled again a day or two later, and again the day after that—bumping their fuzzy little heads on the right-hand side once more. Blast, when *will* this thing settle into place? Only when the beekeeper decides to leave it put.

But suppose you want to move the hive some distance away, maybe a mile or more. Are you going to pursue this inch-along course? Not on your life. Rather, with a couple of nails, you'll knock a length of wood in place over the hive's main entrance to seal it (at night, when the bees are all inside), stuff the upper entrance—a hole about the size of a quarter that's been drilled into the top of the upper box, or "super"—with a rag, hoist the thing onto the back of your pickup truck, and drive off. Having re-sited the hive in an entirely different area, you then free the entrances once more, taking care to reduce the bottom one with a handful of grass or leaves, whatever's handy. This the bees will eventually push to the ground, out of their way; but meanwhile, with the configuration of their primary entrance temporarily altered, they've gotten an important message: something about their situation has fundamentally changed. Now the field bees will take the time and trouble to reorient themselves to the new location—again, with respect to the sun's position in the sky and a couple of nearby landmarks, such as certain trees or boulders—before taking off. And because you've driven them a considerable distance from their previous site, they'll not recognize enough familiar terrain to risk falling into an old flight pattern and inadvertently returning to the old homestead.

We'd been in slow, careful motion maybe eight or ten seconds when Nettie stepped back from the wagon to retrieve the cinder blocks that would need to be set up in the new spot. To free her hands she laid the flashlight down—which was about when Mark yelped in the dark and jerked one hand away from the hive. I barely had time to understand before it suddenly seemed we were all yelping and leaping back from the wagon and shouting expletives. An odd odor something like overripe bananas broke abruptly into the thick summer night, as if released from a jar, and we four capable, rational adults broke into a blind, clumsy run, fleeing countless angry, invisible needles on the wing. Ordinarily even angry bees won't follow you terribly far, but these girls wouldn't settle for ordinary, oh no. I didn't see Jamey or Nettie make it to their cabin, but anyone within a mile heard them thrashing and crashing through their neck of the woods, a tiny beam of light bouncing wildly along somewhere in that direction. Mark and I did our own share of crashing through trees and underbrush—forget trying to find the path, under the circumstances—swearing and swatting to raise the dead. Tumbling through our front door, we slapped our bare arms, the backs of our necks and knees for several minutes beyond what was necessary, unable to shake the sensation they were still coming at us. Even their fierce, electric buzz seemed to linger in the air about our ears.

Any woman of reasonable intelligence would have taken a lesson on such an occasion, if not from those charging battalions then surely from the unhappy, whose-bright-idea-was-this? expression on her husband's face, now swelling from a nasty red sting on the nose. "Reasonably intelligent" aren't the first words people would use to describe me, perhaps. I was hooked. Call it adrenaline surge, call it honeybee venom in my veins—whatever the explanation, henceforth I would need these funky little critters in my life. Givers of sweet, thick honey, bringers forth of the fruits from trees and bushes and who knew what else, they also gave more food for thought than a body could know what to do with, year after year, beginning with this item: not *all* honeybees are afraid of the dark.

The bees that chased and found us that night died in the name of, well, homeland security: feeling their house suddenly sprout feet and begin to move, they determined to stop the giants responsible for so rude a dislocation; just after stinging us, they would have tried to pull away, but their stingers would have caught in our hides so completely that the bees essentially disemboweled themselves by the force of the effort. Which also explains the ripe-banana smell: it results whenever physical injury is done to a bee, serving as a kind of alarm to rouse the rest of the colony.

The little buggers that chased but did not find us that night may also have died for their trouble, though more slowly. The black night prevented them from knowing where they were, and thus from making their way back home, at least till morning. For the most part, honeybees need the sun to steer by. What matters most is its azimuth, its compass direction. The bees can tell east from west, north from south, even on cloudy days, as long as the cloud cover is not unduly thick. Here's how: polarized light waves emitted by the sun are not affected by thin cloud cover, whereas the sun's ordinary light waves are. Unlike mere human eyes, the honeybees' compound eyes (indeed, the eyes of many, many insects) can distinguish polarized from ordinary light waves—and oh, what a world of difference this ability makes for honeybee navigation. Whereas ordinary light waves scatter outward in multiple directions, giving no clue as to their point of origin, the waves in a beam of polarized light travel along a single plane, in effect always pointing backward to the cannon's mouth, the sun itself. So: should you ever become disoriented in the woods on a cloudy day sans compass, the way out of your predicament is simple: just ask a bee, or an ant, or a beetle which way is north.

Besides the sun and landmarks in the vicinity of their hive, bees also orient themselves in the world by their sense of smell, substituting two antennae for our one nose. Their olfactory sense is about as strong as ours with respect to the aromas of nearly everything but flowers, wax, sugar, and other things necessary to their well-being, which they can perceive far more readily than we can. And as if all this navigational equipment weren't enough, honeybees have another, still mysterious faculty: the ability to sense the earth's magnetic field.

For our basic understanding of all honeybee orientation devices except this last, we have primarily to thank the experiments of the Austrian entomologist Karl von Frisch, conducted in the first half of the twentieth century. (Reading his delightful account of these efforts, *The Dancing Bees,* one gets the feeling his were the best-fed honeybees for miles around, since in the course of his experiments he trained and retrained them constantly to dozens of petri dishes full of sugar water.) Von Frisch is justifiably famous not only for his discoveries about honeybee biology and behavior, but also for the charm with which he presents them. Take, for example, the notion of "flower constancy." This refers to the tendency of any given foraging bee to stick to one type of flower for days on end, even if the nectar in her particular flower isn't flowing as strongly as it is for another type growing all around. Having memorized the smell of, say, clover, she will return day after day to that stand of clover until its nectar fades entirely away. Does this mean the nectar welling up from nearby dandelions goes untapped? Not at all. The clover-constant bee can rest assured she's got hundreds, perhaps thousands, of sisters wildly devoted to dandelions, till death (or nectar depletion) do they part. This is all to the good, and not just for the bees—who waste no time each morning trying to make up their minds what they're hungry for, setting out instead directly toward their adopted feeding range—but also, naturally, for the flowers, which depend on the bees to move their pollen around. After all, what's a sprig of clover going to do with dandelion pollen besides spit it out? This business of flower constancy, then, is truly world-formative, helping to ensure that clover pollen gets spread out among clover flowers and dandelion pollen among dandelion flowers, which in turn means the bees— and you and me and my little brown mutt—will long enjoy more of both.

At least one more of Von Frisch's observations concerning honeybee orienteering bears remarking. He wasn't the first to notice that worker bees who are about to take up the foraging stage of their lives first spend a few days making very short orientation flights from their hives and back again, hovering for minutes at a time in front of the box while facing it. But with his petri dishes full of sugar water, Von Frisch was the one who got to the bottom of this curious behavior, finding that bees do not really memorize location as they depart a place but rather when they *return to it*. Like a visitor in a foreign land stepping out of his hotel and looking back to fix its location with respect to the surroundings, Von Frisch points out, the novice honeybee forager has to play at returning for some time in order to fully get her bearings. The moral of the story: she who neglects to spend some time looking backward is soon a doomed honeybee.

Now it must be admitted that metaphors are my weakness, especially the ones tending toward exempla. I'm prone to seeing them everywhere, most particularly in bee behavior. This business of looking backward, for instance, to get one's bearings. Here I sit in the comfortable study of a stone cottage in the heart of this big, improbable continent, trying the backward glance on for size. A biblical rain rages outside, threatening to bring the Arkansas River rather closer to me than its usual five miles. In the pounding monotony it is easy to sit still, here at the threshold of middle age, looking back to a most significant, life-shaping time that was upon me, a time when honeybees caught the eye, and the mind caught fire. A time when I didn't know how thoroughly many other crucial tastes were taking hold in me as well, tastes that now drive my days, in everything from landscapes (rural, foothillish, and edged with water) to flowers (little blue ones, or white), from houses (old) to furniture (old), and from paintings (intelligent, carefully composed) to music to literature (ditto). Happily married at the time, I internalized as well a taste for a certain kind of man: a lot like him, though that is at least as scary as it is a welcome thought, given his difficulties with, ah, flower constancy. Applying the honeybee lesson in orienteering a little more closely, I think about the places, the locales— the hive sites, as it were—that preceded my recent landing in this odd little out-of-the-way spot, this stretch of flatland just east of the Ozarks. Central North Carolina, rural Maine, northern and coastal Mississippi, parts of Maryland, Virginia, Louisiana, and Texas have been home at one time or another, some for several years running. But sometimes I think I catch a ray of polarized light shot in my direction, as if to help me steer through the world, from that slim divide in a patch of Carolina woods, where a bit of sun gets through even on cloudy days.

II.

To open a hive is to pour sunlight upon a wondrous world of miniature jewels shining black and amber, virtually all of them in motion. It's as utterly fantastic a sight as it is common (to a beekeeper, anyway), and therefore oxymoronic in the way of all ordinary miracles—stars spangling a night sky, seeds spiraling across a fat sunflower, ripples shooting through a squirrel's tail. Of course, much of the excitement inherent to opening a hive lies in its power to scare you witless: one heck of a lot of these buzzing little demons appear suddenly before you, nearly all of them equipped to stab painfully. Indeed, as a fiercely loyal family, they might think nothing of mounting a fatal assault, should you make one seriously wrong move.

And early on in your beekeeping career, you're pretty sure you'll make that very move any minute.

So one approaches the inner sanctum of the colony respectfully, deferentially, hat in hand. Or rather, with the darn thing clamped tight to your head, and for Pete's sake be sure it's got a brim wide enough to make a heavy nylon veil fall away from your face and neck. If two stand ready to open the hive but with only one hat-and-veil combo between them, then it will likely go to the apprentice, while the experienced beekeeper manages without. Unless the

beekeeper has recently begun to suspect he's growing allergic to bee sting: that would be Jamey, back in that faraway
dream of a summer. And the bareheaded, noodle-brained
one hanging a couple of feet back, stretching up on her
tippy-toes and leaning in for a glimpse? Right: that would
be me.

But wait: something's *not* right. That is, I can't actually
remember that moment when Jamey introduced me to his
bees. I know he did, I know he gave me my first beekeeping lesson—but the memory is of that sketchy, elusive,
tip-of-the-mind kind. Sunny day—check. Hat and veil on
Jamey—check. The aluminum-clad telescoping cover coming off, followed by the wooden inner cover—check. Those
bronzy-black jewels glinting as if afire, which (I think)
briefly stole my breath. And then, nothing. Dozens upon
dozens of hive openings later, I try to summon that first one
but fail; perhaps the trouble is simply that they all run together now. Maybe it does not matter. Approached in the
right frame of mind, they're always exciting, all the more if
I take my time, without launching too quickly into my inspection or whatever other work I may intend.

Here's how it might have been, way back in the day. I'm
wearing long pants and long sleeves, in light colors if I can
manage it, as I've read (or Jamey's told me) that bees find
lighter colors soothing. Jamey towers a foot above me, and
characteristically speaks very little. We both have on gloves,
mine just cotton gardener's gloves, his a heavier canvas
kind that reach up to his forearms. The hive's top cover,
called a telescoping cover for the way it fits snugly over
both the inner cover and the top edge of the hive box, slips

off easily; this Jamey rests on the ground, upended and
leaning against the back of the hive. Not many bees in sight
just yet, not till we get beyond the inner cover; I can only
just hear them. He picks up his smoker, a metal can with a
squeezable bellows attached in which he has made a small
fire with dried leaves and then cooled the fire off with a few
blades of green grass. (For reasons not entirely understood,
smoke tends to calm honeybees.) Like a priest with his
censer, Jamey points the top of the smoker at the top of the
hive, directing little puffs of pale smoke into an oblong
hole in the center of the inner cover, and again along its
edges as he begins to pry it up with his hive tool. This
handy little item—perhaps the only tool just about any
beekeeper would likely say he could not do without—is a
steel blade about eight or ten inches long and about an
eighth of an inch thick, made for just such occasions: hive
inspection requires a fair amount of prying, in several
senses of the word. Not that the cover is nailed down or
anything. It sticks all along the edges because the bees have
weatherproofed their home, using the gummy brown paste
called propolis that they've made out of various plant
resins they've been collecting, a paste that hardens somewhat as it dries. A little more prying, a few more puffs of
smoke—these from me now, Jamey having suggested I
needn't just stand there—and the inner cover comes away.

    With their roof suddenly gone and the upper floor of
their chamber drenched in unaccustomed sunlight, the bees
pitch their buzzing up a note and a decibel or two; we
stand still. To my great relief, the buzzing dies swiftly back
to its more usual, contented hum. Several bees lift up into

the air to check out the strange new roofless situation; others stroll about the top bars of the ten hanging frames of honeycomb, their bodies catching and throwing back the bright light. The great majority of the colony crawls over the comb slowly and randomly (or so it seems; I'll later learn otherwise), up and down between the frames, while others move more at a run, stopping now and then to pivot and run the other way. Jamey begins easing two frames apart with his hive tool—the propolis seals them together along their top bars where wood meets wood. Soon he has a frame loose, and with another tool, a lightweight, steel grip that handily pinches a top bar more finely than gloved fingers can manage, he pulls the frame up and out of the hive, into the light for examination.

Though dozens of bees cover the comb, a pattern across it quickly comes into view. To begin with, all along the top and a little down the sides, Jamey points out, there appears an arched band of capped honey. Which is to say, ripe honey sealed with a thin and slightly wrinkled layer of ivory-colored wax, so thin you can tell there's something liquid lying underneath; it looks as wax paper might look when covering a brim-full jar of syrup, or, well, you know—honey. Just below these cells and similarly arched are a couple of bands of uncapped cells oozing something amber and wet—nectar that's not yet honey—ordinarily colorless in itself but appearing tinted now with the reddish-gold hue of the wax compartments holding it. A little lower down the comb, we come to several rows of cells plugged with something opaque, in various shades of yellow and orange, and, it seems, a bit gooey: pollen, which the bees will snack on periodically but more often feed to their growing young. And below the pollen—occupying roughly the lower middle of the comb in a sort of oval—lie cells capped with a tan crust of wax, some of the cappings protruding with blunt little butts. All of these contain brood, says Jamey, baby bees going through pupation; the bigger ones—a little too big for their cells and therefore sticking out farther than the rest—are the boys, the drones. Jamey eases this frame of bees and its goods down to the ground, leaning it against the two covers that rest against the hive. (Even after so many years of doing this myself, I'm still awed by the fact that relatively few bees drop or fly off a removed frame, despite its being held up by a large creature in a funny hat, turned this way and that, and then set on the ground. It's as though nothing short of violence of some kind is going to distract those girls from their work.) With one frame out of the way now, Jamey can get to others in the hive a little more comfortably, since nine frames do not fill the box so completely as ten. He pries another one loose, gets a good hold on it with his frame grip, and— Oops, he squashes a bee with one of the pincers, yet its nearby sisters seem hardly to notice their injured, squirming comrade. He lifts this frame to the light as he did the first. It looks much the same, except that I now see scattered near the middle some open cells occupied by fat little curls of white tucked deep inside, some bigger (older, Jamey explains) than others: larvae. These, too, are baby bees, still young enough to need feeding by the house bees, not yet ready to pupate, and therefore not yet sealed with wax.

And then the coolest part of all. Come closer, Jamey urges, turning the frame a little this way and that to get the light on it just right. Closer, come on. (Easy for him to say, in his hat and veil.) There, look . . . just . . . there, he's saying now. With one corner of his hive tool he's pointing at empty cells, so I'm confused and squinting hard everywhere else, till he says, See? Way back against the wall of the cell, do you see a sort of tiny white comma? No-o-o . . . then, Oh yes! Okay, yes, there seem to be a lot of them, one to a cell, each affixed to the back wall, looking very much like white commas on parchment, though larger and less curvy, maybe more like uncooked grains of rice.

Eggs, freshly deposited.

Which means *she* may be nearby—and she is. There, near the bottom of the comb, just pulling her head out of a cell she's been inspecting, rests the queen, long of abdomen but short of wing, dark and heavy looking, pulling behind her as if with some effort the black, gravid body that represents her colony's future. She's flanked all around by six or eight bees with their heads up close to her body—nurse bees following her every move, attending to her every need. Quickly yet gingerly, Jamey eases this frame back into place inside the hive. Because some bees do commonly drop to the ground while one handles a frame of honeycomb, it wouldn't do to let *that* one fall off and risk stepping on her. The colony has but the one queen, so if something happens to her—ooh la, let's not even go there.

On second thought, let's go there. After all, it happens: the beekeeper accidentally injures or kills her while he's knocking about the hive's innards, or a bird nabs her before she can make it back to the hive from her mating flight, taken in the first few days after her birth, or the worker bees themselves kill her off when they sense she's running out of gas—running low on eggs—at three or four years of age. However it happens, facts is facts: the hive is occasionally queenless, or to use the technical term, in deep doo-doo.

It happened with my very first batch of my own bees, and entirely by my own hand. Maybe some part of me wanted to bring on, right at the start, one of the worst situations a beekeeper can face, just to get it out of the way. If there exists somewhere a list of wrong moves a bee-keeper can make, "killing the only queen you've got" appears right up there near the top.

Bear with me here a moment, as a little background is in order.

"Allison! Al-li-son!" Nettie's scream broke the chill, Saturday morning quiet as she came running down the path from her cabin toward mine, flannel bathrobe flying out behind her. "Help me!" The woods still late-winter leafless, I saw her easily through our glass solarium and jumped for the door. She didn't give me a chance to ask what the trouble was—as soon as I appeared she skidded to slow herself, still twenty yards away, turned, and ran back to her place, sure I'd catch up, which I aimed quickly to do. Mark was asleep; for Nettie's wild alarm—unlike anything I'd ever seen in her—there could be only one reason: something had happened to Jamey. A scary thought shot through me: We're way out here in the sticks—how can we get serious

medical attention in time? And this: Nettie is a *nurse*, yet look at her, she's in a total panic.

Expecting to see blood, maybe lots of it—flashing on an old memory of my brother's encounter with an ax when we were small—I took a breath as I raced up the steps and into the house. And there Jamey lay, on his back on the rug just a few feet from the door, stirring a little and, it appeared, trying to wake up. In jeans but shirtless, with no blood in sight. He simply looked like his long-legged slender self, with a generous shock of brown hair, except that he was on the floor. Nettie was on her knees at his side, her sandy hair falling loose from the casual knot she must have put it in when she'd climbed out of bed. On a small wooden table nearby, the eggy leavings of their breakfast lay abandoned. Jamey seemed groggy but not otherwise altered; Nettie urged him to lie back down—he'd begun to sit up—and he complied. Somewhat encouraged yet also bewildered (and still on the lookout for blood), I wondered what had given Nettie such a fright and what she seemed to think I could do about it.

The answer to the second never came, but the answer to the first came quickly: pulling on a T-shirt that he'd taken off their clothesline the day before, Jamey had been stung in the center of his chest by a wasp lurking in the folds (now I saw the reddening welt). One surprised cry later, the shirt was off again and on the floor, the wasp crushed by an annoyed stomp, and Jamey was reaching for the drawer where he kept his EpiPen. He had just time enough to use it before he felt funny, saw the room spin, and followed his shirt and attacker to the floor. Nettie flew to the phone to call the county paramedics, then raced out the door to rouse me.

At least some mild allergic reaction to bee or wasp sting is normal in just about everybody—think back to your own experiences, often had in childhood: some localized redness and swelling, a right smart burning feeling for an hour or more, and itching for a day or so. Multiple stings incurred all at once can put enough venom into a person to cause more serious problems, even death. (These instances are rare, fortunately, but it's good to know about them, so you'll stay in your car if, for example, you ever come upon an overturned pickup truck that has scattered its cargo of beehives across the road.) Of greater concern is that small percentage of the population with an especially strong sensitivity to insect sting, people for whom even one sting could be fatal. This is what so undid Nettie that Saturday morning, the fear that Jamey had, when he fainted, gone into anaphylactic shock (the sting's proximity to his heart didn't help matters, in her view). Anaphylaxis is a severe allergic reaction that can quickly—within as little as fifteen minutes—shut down a person's respiratory and circulatory systems. Because Jamey'd already had a close call in the recent past, a doctor had prescribed the EpiPen, a little syringe full of epinephrine designed in such a way as to let even a novice self-administer a shot right after a sting. Epinephrine is an adrenal hormone that counters the body's decidedly overzealous attempts to ward off the allergen (the insect poison) by, in effect, committing suicide.

Tending to him now—mostly I just stood there trying to think what I could do, while Jamey gradually came to his senses—Nettie could see that the EpiPen had done its job, that he was probably going to be fine, though he'd need to take it easy for the rest of the day. She felt a bit sheepish about having run for me, apparently realizing for the first time that her usual self-confidence as a nurse could evaporate when the victim was one of her own. We had to laugh, if a little nervously, at the faint wail we now heard beyond the woods. The siren of an ambulance, wandering lost among the country roads.

Thus it came to pass that Jamey consigned to me his beehive and a short introductory book he owned on beekeeping. Suddenly I felt the weight of a tender responsibility: all those little *lives* now lay in my care. The bees themselves promptly cured this sentimentality by dying— every last one of them—before I could even begin to acquaint them with their new guardian. One day not long after Jamey's own brush with the Reaper, I donned hat, veil, gloves, long pants, and long sleeves, and carefully opened the hive as I'd watched Jamey do, sweating with nerves. And got no reaction from the bees whatsoever. The hive—the same one that had sent four of us running and yelling like banshees that moonless night months before— had become a morgue.

Oh my, what a shame. The scene within bore no resemblance to that glorious one Jamey had shared with me the previous summer. Safe to remove gloves and veil, anyway, so as to get a better look, and safe to ask Jamey to examine the situation and help me understand, if possible, what had happened. Whereas the honeycomb in the frames should have been a vibrant tan and chocolate brown (it darkens as it ages, from constant bee traffic), and whereas it should have been covered with roaming bees, everything now was a dull battleship gray and a little dusty, as if some of the wax had dried and flaked into dandruff. What bees there were lay dead and desiccated all across the hive floor in a layer an inch or more thick, and in a handful of cells, their bodies just emerging headfirst, as though death had caught them at the very moment of their being born. Jamey wasn't able to say for sure what could have brought this on; he suspected mites, either one of two in particular that had recently become newsworthy among American bee-keepers. The tracheal mite (*Acarapis woodi*) invades a bee's trachea, punctures it, and sucks on its blood; *Varroa destructor,* usually just called Varroa, feeds on pupating larvae and adult bees, which can lead to such physiological malformations as undersized wings. Both types spread fairly easily from one hive to another. Although one or the other (or both) is by now likely to be present to some de-gree in any colony at any given time, a heavy infestation of either can doom a colony, especially in late winter when its population is naturally at its lowest ebb. If the hive doesn't have enough healthy workers on hand to get its many chores done when spring commences, it's essentially a goner.

Well then, I'll just start over, I decided. Using a beekeeping-supply catalog of Jamey's, I ordered fresh woodenware—precut pieces of pine with which to make new frames—and beeswax foundation, as it wouldn't do to use the old stuff, in case it harbored disease. I also or-dered my first package of bees, an amusing idea in itself, that one can—with just a phone, a credit card, and the co-operation of the United States Postal Service—conjure up a little self-contained community of living animals. When the post office called a few days later to say my bees had arrived, and would I *please* make haste to retrieve them, I was in the car in two shakes. What's commonly termed a "package" of bees is actually a small cage, maybe a foot long and half as wide, with wooden ends and sturdy, small-meshed wire screen making up the four sides. Thousands of little black feet, tongues, and antennae fur the screened sides as the bees constantly try to make sense of their situation. (They can't sting through the wire mesh, but knowing that doesn't take away much of the suspense you feel while handling their cage.) Honeybees are sold by the pound, and though a few die in transit, most of them, around ten or twelve thousand, make the trip and land in your hands distinctly less than happy about their coach-class accommodations. For the journey they've been provided, attached to one end of their cage, a small can of sugar syrup with very small punctures allowing honeybee tongue access; since this food may be depleted by the time they reach their destination, the buyer is urged to sprinkle them, through the wire mesh, with a little fresh water in which some sugar has been dissolved. Licking this treat off one another will help revive them and take their minds briefly off the fact that they're still hiveless. Also attached to the inside of the cage is a much smaller, additional cage, in which travel a mated queen (one ready to begin laying eggs as soon as she's freed) and a few attendant bees. The queen and all the other bees in the package did not necessarily—did not likely—come from the same original hive in the supplier's apiary or "beeyard," so this cage-within-a-cage arrangement gives them all a chance to become acquainted during their trip, but does not allow the several thousand worker bees complete access to her. This is important because bees will often kill a queen that's strange to them (by "balling" her, that is, surrounding and suffocating her) if they can get at her; if they can't, and if their own queen is nowhere in sight—or rather, nowhere in smell—then gradually they will grow accustomed to this new gal's perfume and decide she's their queen.

So how does one get from this odd little three-pound batch of fellow insect travelers to an active honeybee hive? Slowly, gingerly.

Having let the cage rest for a day or so in a cool, dark space, as directed—I chose the cabinet underneath my kitchen sink; tempted a couple of times to open it and check on everybody, I was greeted by a slight amplification of their collective buzzing, as the light fell on them—I took the cage, my protective headgear, and a claw hammer (for prying the cage open) all out to the garden in the power cut, where the vacant hive lay waiting. I'd read over and over the section of my introductory book on installing package bees to be sure I knew what to do. (No use asking Jamey's advice; he'd inherited his hive already full of bees from someone else.) First, open the wooden end that will give you access to the queen cage, and remove that. A few worker bees will begin to escape, but that's okay—they won't go far. With a nail or a small pocketknife, pry out the little piece of cork plugging the hole at one end of the queen cage; with the cork gone, a second plug made of soft candy becomes visible. This the bees will chew away, eventually yielding an exit for the queen and her attendants. Until such time as they manage it, the queen cage should hang, candy side up, between two frames of beeswax foundation within the hive. To secure it in place I simply wedged it between the wooden top bars of these adjacent frames, which turned out not to be good enough, as I suspect you'll agree shortly. The next step is the exciting (read unnerving) part: after opening the cage proper, you do your best to dump the bees all at once into the hive from above, shaking the cage so as to make the laggards drop out of it. They won't all cooperate, so after you've closed the hive you'll need to lay the open cage on the ground in front of the bottom-board entrance and cross your fingers that these last several dozen bees head in to join their sisters before nightfall, which they very likely will.

Then you go away, leaving everybody alone for a while to set up house—and this I did, hugely relieved I hadn't been stung. Within three or four days it's time to check on them, most particularly to make sure that wax honeycomb is being "drawn out"—that the flat sheets of factory-fresh wax you provided are being transformed into three-dimensional, hexagonal apartments—and that the queen has been released. And this, too, I did—discovering, to my horror, that the cage had fallen to the hive floor with the queen still in it, deader than dead. *Candy side up*: I suddenly remembered the instructions for how to orient her little cage relative to the hive. I'd placed it candy side down, so that when the pressure created by the two frames holding it aloft relaxed ever so slightly, the cage plummeted straight to the floor and remained upright, held in that position by the closeness of the frames on either side. The candy-plugged hole had become entirely inaccessible to the house bees. With no way to release the queen, the little would-be colony was unable to save her.

That now became the thing in need of saving: the colony itself. Comb was being drawn out, and some foraging for groceries had begun, but even as this nation-building was picking up steam, a handful of bees were dying daily from natural causes and no new bees were on the way, as there'd been no eggs laid. No eggs in a hive means no future, no young workers in the pipeline to replace the older bees as they die off.

It happens that evolution has tried to answer this contingency, but hasn't yet succeeded among most races of honeybees. In a queenright colony—one with a healthy, laying queen present—the bees cannot help spreading their lady's unique scent, her pheromone, among themselves in the course of their activities. One of the many effects of the pheromone's presence is to suppress development of the workers' ovaries; remember, these girls *are* girls, born with girlish organs, never mind that those organs are nonfunctional 99.9 percent of the time. It's that .1 percent that my nascent colony found itself faced with when I accidentally killed their queen and inadvertently halted her production of perfume. Unless I provided them with another queen fast, some of these workers would develop functioning ovaries and actually begin laying eggs. There you have it, nature trying to come to the rescue—except that the plan still needs some fine-tuning. At this point in their evolutionary history, worker bees that lay eggs produce only drones—males who will prove unable to build comb, clean out the hive, or forage for supplies. Or, obviously, lay eggs. All they know how to do is eat honey and go flying off periodically in search of queens with which to mate. So again: the future could hold for such a hive only no worker eggs, which is to say, no future at all. One South African race of honeybee, *Apis mellifera capensis,* has mastered the trick of getting female eggs out of laying workers, from which a new queen can be raised. But most honeybee workers that become layers can produce nothing but males.

My new little colony, then—my first, my own!—was on a crash course unless something was done, and fast.

Supply catalog, phone, credit card, and Postal Service all went into concerted action once more, and two days later I had another queen accompanied by several attendant bees. Into the hive with her cage—candy side *up*—and the day was saved. Until the following winter, when I lost the entire colony, again most probably to mites.

Buddhists teach the value of detachment, which Westerners sometimes mistake for indifference. I certainly did, upon first encountering the notion. Detachment, however, isn't about not caring what happens; it's about not letting what happens knock you down too hard, or for too long. About realizing that your need to control outcomes is often bound to meet with disappointment and cost you suffering—unnecessary suffering, because anything more than a modicum of control in virtually any situation is illusory to begin with. "Happiness isn't getting what you want, but wanting what you get," reads a T-shirt my husband gave me, who knows why. Far more easily said than practiced, of course, for instance when what you've got is yet another dead beehive. Still, detachment in the face of failure is helpful, if one would take up beekeeping: honeybees are animals, living and working in close proximity to other animals and plants, all of whom are constantly striving to have their day in the sun, to be all that they can be in their short lives. (Many, many of these beings die without achieving much beyond serving as food to another creature—an honor every single one of them, and each of us, eventually fulfills.) Then along you come, yet another animal with a plan of your own, to get a share of the sweetness coaxed into the world by sun and rain, collected by insects and subsequently rendered into honey. But neither the bees, nor the mites, flowers, soil, microbes, and worms, nor the wind, water, and sun, nor anything else in creation has any special reason to cooperate with this or any other of your nifty schemes, never mind that you're so smart and lovable and eminently deserving. So it will not do to be too thoroughly put out or put off by failure, a certain amount of which is inevitable in beekeeping, as in all forms of that universally chancy business we call agriculture.

Of course, if you're trying to make a living at it, there may come a point when too much failure gets expensive. A hobbyist, too, risks approaching an unbearable lightness of the pocketbook, so before that day arrives she must do her best to master her own animal role among these fascinating animals and plants, if she hopes to participate season after season in the great, intricate, partially but never fully knowable ecological dance in which they are engaged. That, or surrender the floor to more capable partners.

And surrender I did, for a short while anyway. By the following spring I had successfully interviewed for my first faculty appointment, effective in August but contingent upon my having the Ph.D. in hand. Which suddenly made the little matter of an unfinished dissertation into a rather bigger matter. Swallowing hard, I put out of my head all thoughts of keeping bees or even planting a garden that season, so as to force myself to stay at my desk the better part of every day. Now and then I emerged from our cabin to roam the woods, mentally girding my loins for the coming goodbye, since the job I had landed would move us hundreds of miles, to rural Maine. A big part of me didn't want to go: "Carolina is my home," I found myself whispering up into the swaying, uninterested pines, deliberately mouthing the title of a Charles Kurault coffee-table number featuring sumptuous pictures of the Tarheel State. Another part of me was eager for the adventure: *"Maine!"* this Southern girl whispered. "We're bound for snow country, Ben!" He sat up attentively and cocked his head my way. Resting on the stump where Jamey had taught me how to split firewood, I told my dog as much as I thought I knew. The famously cold, pink-and-umber rocky coast smelling smartly of oceanic life and death, the big old New England–postcard barns, the black boreal forests. Foxes loping across meadows whitened by frost. Loons calling from the shadowy edges of twilit ponds.

But the very biggest part of me simply did not want to stay behind at the university, among other recently minted Ph.D.s whose sagging shoulders, unpaid student loans, and failure to secure faculty posts became the grist of grad-student gossip around town. Flopping at beekeeping I could face; failing to turn my many years of school into a respectable job was something else entirely. I did not yet recognize—or at least did not yet chafe about—the community-killing nature of the whole business of academic hiring, which shares with corporate culture an indifference to place, to any notion of human rootedness. To launch my career I had to apply for openings all over the country, aware that if anything came of the effort I might have to move far away—and to convince my husband to leave a place and some neighbors he'd grown to love, despite his original reluctance to take up life in the woods at all. He agreed eventually to the move north; only much later would I fully realize what that decision cost him, and what it was to cost me.

For now, careerism was in the air, sweeping me up and away like a kite cut loose, more or less happily loose, truth be told. Besides. Surely they had gardens and beehives in Maine, too. Right? Or they would when I got there.

3

Go Forth and Be Fruitful

Concerning a swarm of bees
Take earth in your right hand
Cast it under your right foot and say
I have it underfoot; I have found it.
Behold earth avails against all kinds of creatures
It avails against malice and evil jealousy
And against the mighty tongue of man.

When they swarm scatter earth over them and say
Alight victorious women, alight on the earth
Never turn wild and fly to the woods
Be just as mindful of my benefit
As is every man of his food and his fatherland.

   —ANONYMOUS MEDIEVAL CHARM, ENGLAND;

     translated by Kevin Crossley-Holland

I.

They're a form of livestock, honeybees are, but I'll grant you that's an odd idea. You don't toss hay for them, erect expensive water tanks, or set up feeding troughs; you don't tag their ears (do bees have ears?), rope and wrestle them to the ground, or brand their rumps. You don't dip them in pesticide, worm them, shear their coats, or rise at three in the morning to help one get born. You don't milk them twice daily or track their progress toward market weight. You don't need (thank the gods) a "nutrient management plan"—a strategy for disposing of their wastes. You don't need to own any land or provide any pasture—beehives are kept well nigh everywhere, including city rooftops, even atop the Paris Opera House—though it's true that bees in a rural area where there's little aerial spraying of poisons will generally prosper, frequently outperforming a town hive. As for building them stalls or a barn: the closest you come is knocking together some simple pine boxes with removable wooden frames. In lieu of straw bedding you provide flat, fragrant sheets of beeswax (one sheet per frame) that have been mechanically embossed with a uniform honeycomb pattern, to encourage comb-building by the power of suggestion.

Most remarkable of all, you don't fence them in, these daughters of the pioneers (and I do mean pioneers; more on this shortly). You *want* them to get out, to race off, to run wild and plunder the neighbors' fields and gardens, for among livestock, bees alone are always free-range. But you also want them to come back: a shameless plantation overseer, you think of your bees as field hands harvesting a crop, and by golly it had better all come home each evening where it belongs, in those hive boxes you lovingly built and painted and furnished, and which you fully intend to rob someday soon of their treasure.

So it's clear enough why we don't call it bee farming or

bee ranching. But why bee*keeping*? Search me. Perhaps this "keeping" of quasi-wild animals bears some resemblance to a man's keeping of a mistress. Like a mistress, a honeybee sticks around only so long as you suffer her demands for cozy quarters, ensure her access to rich foods, and give her enough time alone to cultivate the delusion that she's living her days mostly to please herself.

But oh, what sadness if ever she should decide circumstances aren't to her liking, and without so much as a thank-you or goodbye she flees the scene, just vanishes! In the beekeeper's case, multiply that loss of one lovely darling by several thousand, and then have the tact to avert your gaze from his desolate countenance.

My own reaction to my first swarm was less poetic. Dang. Oh my. They're *leaving*! Somebody call 911, call out the militia, do something! Of course, living in rural Maine at the time and married to a guy who had decided bees were for the birds, I was the only somebody within earshot, and supposedly the only somebody around with half a clue what was happening, let alone any clue what to do about it. Not that any of that made any difference: they swarmed, I stared, and we parted ways forever.

A bright summer's day, say about noon. Hanging wet laundry on the line out back, thinking of little more than whether I'll have enough pins for the job. A breeze picks up just behind me—no, make that around me—wait, what weird wind *is* this, gathering speed, whipping about, thrumming with some strange, insistent murmur? Dropping a sock and pivoting about in midstoop, I register the situation: this isn't empty air swirling around, these are bees, and not just the usual few at a time taking off to forage. We're talking thousands of bees, flying oddly in concert. And oh great Caesar's ghost, I'm wearing only shorts and a tank top. Dashing for the safety of our screened back porch, just about thirty feet away, I feel dozens of bugs bump me and careen briefly off course. Hot as the day is, my skin prickles with an allover chill at the thought of my close call; at this time, I share with most of the untutored the erroneous notion that a swarm is a mass of angry bees. Easy enough to make that mistake, as they certainly fly with fierce energy and purpose, so fast you can't quite see any of them singly, just the blur of their collective passing. From the porch I hug myself to calm down and watch the maelstrom shrink inward, appearing to gain speed the way water rolling around the sloped sides of a metal basin will quicken as it approaches the drain. And then, marvel to beat all marvels, the great spinning cloud attenuates further, actually taking coherent shape in midair even as it moves away from the clothesline and up several feet. A bronze cone materializes within seconds, nose pointed earthward, with a branch of our biggest, oldest apple tree running through its thick top.

The wind this crowd stirred up now fades, as does their buzzing. The swarm has led its queen to that branch and clustered heavily around her, thousands of bees clinging to one another and hanging two, now three feet down, the bottommost ones losing their grip temporarily and dripping off very much as honey itself might, catching themselves on a draft of air and flying back up again. It's a living cornucopia, it's a molten flow, why, it's—

It's half my dad-gum livestock, that's what it is, and did I mention as well a fat share of the honey harvest, tucked away in their gazillions of bulging bellies? Food for the road, and for the first few days of home-building in a new place. All of it way up on a branch too high for me to reach, the way I've read of other beekeepers salvaging a swarm and hiving it, easy as whistling for a dog. And these girls won't be headed home to my hive—my unfenced, un-gated, and unlocked "barn"—by nightfall.

Dang.

And now another curious thing: in the corner of our farmhouse formed by the joining of an ell to the back porch, a couple dozen bees move purposefully all over the cedar shingles, from roof to ground—not flying or hover-ing but walking, almost running, from one crack to an-other, where the shingles meet and overlap. Scouts: the Special Ops team, sent out to look for promising real es-tate. A swarm of bees is one big homeless army in need of new digs, some decently sheltered cavity like a hollow tree or a space between the inner and outer walls of a building. Within a few minutes it's clear these particular scouts are striking out. Others, presumably, are having better luck elsewhere, for soon the bronze cone dissipates and melts out of the apple tree, then slips away like a genie let out of a lamp, undulating into the summer sky over our back pas-ture, becoming finally just a crayon smear headed for the woods. I squint in the direction of my hive, lying a dozen yards or so beyond the apple tree, about where the door-yard ends and the pasture begins: from here I can't tell whether anything about it seems changed, and I'm still not

ready to leave this screened porch for a closer look. Piti-
fully, the bees roaming over the house soldier on right there
for the rest of the day, probably destined to die in the grass
that night.

So what had come over this crew, anyway? Why vacate
a perfectly comfortable home? Several possibilities come
to mind, the most likely being that domestic conditions
had in fact become less than perfect. For just a couple–
three weeks too long, I had let the colony go about its
work undisturbed, and business had been so brisk that
they'd outgrown their hive box, topping—are you sitting
down?—sixty thousand or more. (How do you count sixty
thousand bees? Very, very carefully.) Add to these teeming
numbers a spell of warm, sultry weather heating up the
hive (even Maine gets a few such days now and then) and
the fact that the queen had run low on empty cells to fill
with eggs, and presto-chango, the urge among some of
them to move on had grown irrepressible. A sizable percentage of the colony had swarmed, or, as we sometimes
say, absconded. Had I been paying better attention—had I
stopped to notice the large numbers of bees clinging close
together to the outside of the hive each day like a big
ragged patch on a white sail—I might have prevented this
day's disaster by one of a handful of means. Which really is
to say, had I been an adept beekeeper.

Incompetence has its consolations, now and then a
good story or two. But sometimes you'd just as soon have
the honey.

"Disaster," I'm calling this event, though of course,

from nature's point of view, it was anything but. A swarm represents about half the adult population of the hive (sometimes more), and when it departs it has in mind pretty much what an expanding company in a capitalist economy has in mind: the opening of fresh franchises, in order to exploit new opportunities to do all over again what it does best. (The remaining bees will carry on nicely right where they are, under the reign of a new queen they've raised themselves.) A swarm is *Apis mellifera*'s way of making increase, of spreading its numbers all over the place; of reproducing asexually, as if the queen's prodigious egg-laying were not already sufficient to ensure the colony's genetic legacy; and, possibly, in the process, of edging out the competition—of outperforming other insects in the search for an area's nectar and pollen.

Which brings me to a point in honeybee history that pains me. Among North American insects, and those of other continents beyond its native Africa as well, the honeybee has proven a shameless bully, an uninvited guest that moved in and quickly made itself at home, driving many native insects into a sort of ecological corner from which it can be hard to make a comeback. She hasn't done it by overt aggression; she's done it just by being darn good at her work.

Let's back up a bit. Unbeknownst to and therefore unremarked by most of us most of the time, well over two hundred thousand species of bees, ants, flies, wasps, butterflies, moths, bats, birds, and even some mammals are constantly at work building, through pollination, the natural world as we know it. Nearly all flowering plants—

including many of our trees and most of our food and fiber
crops—must get some help when they set out to have sex
with others of their various tribes. Obviously, when boy
wants to meet girl in the plant world, he can't just mosey
over her way and sidle up real close. While he's stuck in the
ground *here,* she's way over *there*—perhaps only centime-
ters away, but as good as a world apart to any would-be
plant Casanova. So he needs an intermediary, a match-
maker, some sort of courier willing and able to move the
male stuff of new life—pollen—over to waiting female
flowers, through whose pistils the pollen grains will grow
till they reach the ovaries, whereupon seed production can
commence. In many plant species, the male and female
parts exist within a single flower, yet bridging even that in-
finitesimal distance usually requires a go-between. A few
flowering plants routinely self-pollinate, but among angiosperms these represent the radical fringe, solipsists to a
fault. A goodly number of species use wind or water for
pollination assistance, but we're concerned here with the
ones that have learned (so to speak) to put animals to
work, chiefly insects, luring them into service by means of
pretty petals in which to hide from predators or on which
to conduct their own mating, and by sweet fragrances
promising a tiny nectar or pollen snack. (Not too much at
once: that way a visitor has to hit lots of flowers many
times to get its fill.) Although most flowering plants aren't
picky about whom they entice their way, some have "decided," a bit perversely, over the course of millennia that it
is in their interest to specialize in one sort of bug rather
than another. The honeybee is not among this elect com-

pany; she's a generalist, happy to patronize any flower offering a reward that she can actually reach with her comparatively short tongue. Called mutualism, this reciprocal,
back-scratching arrangement between the pollinators and
the pollinated has been eons—or more precisely, about one
hundred twenty million years—in the making.

Few pollinators have succeeded at this game beyond the
level of the honeybee. From its African origins it went on
to conquer all but the northernmost reaches of Asia
and Europe, and from there (with human help) the Ameri-
cas, Australia, and New Zealand. Paradoxically, though,
this very success has tarnished her reputation among entomologists concerned about our increasingly endangered
native pollinators.

When the Europeans came to the New World, they
brought more than iron tools, an appetite for furs, and
smallpox: they also brought *Apis mellifera*. And like me,
one of their own countless progeny, the colonists were
none too good at keeping their colonies of bees down on
the farm. As the settlers themselves swarmed westward, so
did their bees—indeed, owing to the swarm impulse that
naturally arises in most hives at some time or another,
often the bees preceded the pioneers. Among some Native
Americans word was that the sight of a honeybee meant
the white man couldn't be far behind. Untold millions
of swarms now stand between my hives and those of
Jamestown, so it is incorrect to speak of any honeybees
you come upon in the North American wild as being, well,
wild. No, these are feral bees, domestic escapees, or the
offspring thereof. In their book *The Forgotten Pollinators*,

Stephen L. Buchmann and Gary Paul Nabhan explore the question of what the honeybee's spread across the continent has meant to the native pollinating insects. They and their fellow scientists call it "scramble competition": A single nonnative ("exotic") species moves in on the territory of the natives and shakes things up by more or less taking over the neighborhood, scarfing up so much of the area's resources as to basically eat the locals out of house and home. Like most other exotics, the bees have had a comfortable time of it here, mainly because they have faced so few predators in the woods and enjoyed such abundant supplies in the woodland pantry. By sheer force of numbers, by a workaholic ethos virtually unrivaled in the insect world, and by a tendency to forage heavily just when nectar production tends to peak—early and late in the day— honeybees will sometimes send native bees and other pollinators to bed hungry. Let that happen often enough, and those carpenter bees or bumblebees (or whatever) will raise fewer and fewer young, to the point where their numbers in a given area may be seriously compromised. The arrival of the "white man's fly," then, meant nearly as much bad news for native American pollinators as did the white man himself for Native Americans.

As if this weren't trouble enough for indigenous species, the situation worsened dramatically as human settlement sprawled and agriculture industrialized. Because many of the native species are ground nesters, three centuries of paving over or, alternatively, mechanically cultivating vast tracts of land have left wildlife habitat as fragmented and ragged as a big bolt of rotting cloth. Add to this physical upheaval the heavy chemical treatment—

read "poisoning"—of our land and water over some five or six decades, through pesticide and herbicide applications from the air and on the ground, by farmers, golf-course landscapers, and lawn-loving homeowners, and the upshot could mean only doom for huge populations of resident pollinators. Consider, for example, the hawkmoths that once pollinated the now endangered Antioch Dunes, California, evening primrose: according to Buchmann and Nabhan, nobody's seen a hawkmoth in recent years; nor has anyone seen the particular variety of squash and gourd bee (*Xenoglossa strenua*) that until recently frequented southern Florida's squashes, gourds, and pumpkins; nor very many individuals of the lesser long-nosed bat, formerly a very effective pollinator of saguaro cacti and century plants in the desert Southwest. The list goes on.

The chemical rain has been especially devastating, despite the fact that the majority of affected insects were not the intended targets: pesticides generally don't play favorites, even though the goal may be to nail just one particular pest. Rachel Carson worried over this famously in her 1962 blockbuster *Silent Spring*; however, despite the era of environmental protection ushered in by her elegant plea for saner handling of synthetic poisons, the rain continues to the present, and in greater volumes than in Carson's day.

Well, tough luck, you say. It's a big, cruel world, chock full of even bigger problems than the survival challenges of a few little-known bugs. Good thing we *do* have all those honeybees around now, you say, to take up the slack, to pollinate everything and keep the world turning.

But not so fast: though it's true that honeybees can and

do fill in many gaps when some of the locals are lost—
again, they helped *create* those gaps—they can't do so in
every case. Remember that little matter of *A. mellifera*'s
relatively short tongue? Right: for some flowers, those with
long, tubular corollas, this bug comes packaged in the
wrong anatomy. Lose a few key long-tongued critters, such
as certain butterflies or hummingbirds, and we can probably kiss some of their favorite plant species goodbye as
well.

Or maybe it's not a tongue-length issue, maybe it's a be-
havioral problem. Take the tomato plant, for example, and
its cute little yellow blossom, the one that shows up right
where you're hoping a big beefsteak will soon swell and
droop, heavy and red. Now, this flower produces no nectar, so any visiting insect will be interested solely in its
protein-packed pollen, which is just fine by the tomato
plant. But the pollen grains in that flower aren't accessible
to honeybees, because honeybees don't know how to act
around such a blossom so as to loosen those grains from
their anthers. Whereas the honeybee is your straitlaced,
no-nonsense, just-the-facts-ma'am sort of pollen collector,
the tomato flower requires a more demonstrative bug, one
with a theatrical bent. A bumblebee answers perfectly. Unlike the honeybee, this customer has a trick up its sleeve,
"sonication"; more picturesquely, "buzz pollination." Encountering a tomato blossom full of pollen, the bumblebee
grabs hold of it like a drunk clutching a bar stool, and for
a few seconds she shakes her whole body for all she's
worth, producing a buzzing sound. Not the sound so much
as the actual vibrations cause the pollen grains in the an-
ther to knock into one another, and then to ooze forth, and

finally to burst out in a cloud. The bumblebee gets a drenching (just what she was hoping for) and the flower pollinates its female parts, so fertilization can commence. *Et voilà,* later in the summer big slices of that beefsteak land in your sandwich. Three cheers for the bumblebee!

And tomatoes aren't the only plants that make use of sonication; think eggplant, kiwi, and the berries blue and cran. In other words, stuff we like to eat.

But wouldn't you know, there's still another hitch, one that loops us back around to where we started: bumblebees are among those insects that have lost ground to honeybees in the competition for resources from flowers they both do happen to frequent. Fewer bumblebees means fewer pollinators for plants like tomatoes, which really dig that bee's particular buzz. (Some self-pollination works in tomato flowers as well, but the plants are far more prolific in the company of bumblebees.)

Fortunately, the major fruit and berry crops are happy to entertain honeybee guests when opportunity knocks— with these flowers, there's more than one way, ah, to do it, so they aren't stuck relying on sonicating insects. Indeed, precisely because so many indigenous species like the bumblebee have been depopulated, commercial cranberry and blueberry growers (among others) go in heavily for honeybee pollination, and they do not leave it to chance: either they keep bees themselves in the fields or, more likely, they rent hives from a beekeeper, who schleps them around as the "bloom" of a given crop kicks in. (At last count, fifteen billion dollars' worth of U.S. crops were pollinated each year by honeybees.) And unlike a ground-nesting local, the honeybees can be deliberately placed in a field and later removed, usually by means of a forklift capable of handling a half dozen hives at a time—in synch with spraying regimens, minimizing losses to poisoning. A sizable percentage of commercial beekeepers in turn rely on such partnerships with growers to supplement their income from honey sales, and not incidentally to increase significantly the volume of honey they have to sell. Many of these folks travel the country in eighteen-wheeled flatbed trucks laden with hundreds of hives apiece, moving like migrant farm workers from one crop to another as the seasons and the crops require. (To maximize honey production, they're happy to place hives in the vicinity of wild plants as these come into bloom, too.) In *Following the Bloom,* Douglas Whynott indicates the range of plants serviced and the geographic reaches traversed by migratory beekeepers. The passage is worth quoting in its entirety:

> In America, migratory beekeepers move from Oklahoma, Texas, and Mississippi to Iowa to pollinate apple and pear trees, strawberries and raspberries; they move to the long-grass prairie and the Red River Valley for sunflower, to the Big Horn Valley in Wyoming for alfalfa, to Wisconsin to pollinate apples, to Washington for snowberry and apple and cherry, to Oregon for clover and thistleberry and cherry and vetch, to Ohio for sunflower and apple, from Florida to New York to pollinate apples, from South Carolina to New Jersey to pollinate blueberry and cranberry, from Florida to Pennsylvania to pollinate fruit trees, to Maryland for apple and cherry and tulip poplar and peach, to West Virginia for apple, to

Delaware for lima beans, to Virginia for sourwood and cucumber and melons, to Michigan for cherry and raspberry and blueberry, from Texas and Mississippi to Wisconsin for cranberry and cucumber and apple and cherry, to Colorado for alfalfa and sweet clover, to cantaloupe and tamarack in Arizona, to prickly pear in Utah, to clover and alfalfa in Wyoming, in California to almond orchards and to prune and pear and kiwi, to melon and sunflowers, to orange and to alfalfa, to star thistle and black sage and desert flowers in the Owens Valley, to Idaho for pollination of apple and pear and cherry and vegetable seed, and into West Texas for cotton and alfalfa, to the Rio Grande Valley for marigold, honeydew, squash, cucumber, cantaloupe, and salt cedar, and to the Texas high plains for kinnikinnik, to Florida for citrus and Brazilian pepper bush, mallaluca and palmetto and mango, to Georgia for gallberry and tulip poplar and tupelo and titi, to Massachusetts for apple, to Maine for blueberry, to Cape Cod for cranberry.

As they've done for millennia, then, honeybees still spread themselves all over the place by swarming with some regularity—but now billions of them also get around with a little help from their hardworking, coffee-swilling, pedal-to-the-metal trucker friends.

Well now, look what's happened. A few pages and nearly ten years ago we were way up in Maine, watching half my hive make a beeline for the woods, and somehow we ended

up following the bloom all over creation with those migratory beekeepers. That's how it is when you begin to pay
close attention to honeybees: the next thing you know,
you're studying everything from wildflowers to colonial
settlement patterns to federal price supports for agriculture
(like most commodity food products, honey was on the
government dole up until the late 1990s).

Those bees of mine weren't the only ones trying to improve their domestic arrangements that memorable summer. Having overwintered during our first school year in
Maine in a rental house near the college that had drawn us
north, Mark and I spent free hours in the spring hunting
for a place we could afford to buy on my full-time and his
part-time salary. (Ostensibly, he was still working on the
dissertation he would need to hand in to earn his degree,
but he'd also opted to teach a couple of classes at the college.) The Carolina cabin had given us both a taste for
interesting shelter, but in rural Maine, "interesting" is
code—to a real estate agent, say—for the old adage that
begins, "A fool and his money . . ." We parted company
with our savings to put a down payment on a two-story,
Cape-style farmhouse, its cedar shingles painted a creamy
tan, its trim white, and its front door—rarely opened, as
back doors are commonly favored in the country for every-
day use—a cheerful, welcoming red. The house had once
stood at the center of a small, prosperous dairy operation.
Like so many others of its kind in the region, the farm had
failed in stages, each one marked by the sale, or gift to a
family member, of a portion of the surrounding land, until
all that remained of the original spread was the aging

house, an abandoned barn, and a half dozen acres of meadow, bordered by a moldering rock wall with tall ash, elm, and oak trees growing straight up and out of it. A fine, large stand of lilacs fronted the road near the end of the gravel driveway—not exactly "in the dooryard," where Whitman's famous elegy to the assassinated Lincoln places them, but evocative nevertheless of a bygone era.

Classic New England, in other words, to a pair of greenhorns from the South, where love of ruin is practically bred in the bone.

Well before Mark and I came on the scene, the homestead had passed out of the dairy family entirely (though some of them still lived just up and across the road) and through the hands of others. At some unknown but not too distant point, one of these others had replaced the long, decrepit barn with a more compact and sturdy one, two stories high and smelling sweetly of hay and sawdust, suitable for a couple of horses. And wouldn't you know, a horse was in residence when we took possession of the place: our purchase having caused the unfortunate eviction of a young, renting couple, we thought it the least we could do to let their mottled-white Arabian stay until they could find somewhere else to board him. It proved a more extended stay than we initially imagined, but as long as they provided his grain, we didn't much mind. Big old sixteen-hand Buck had grown all too true to his name and could no longer be ridden by anyone, so we didn't try. Still, he seemed so lonely, racing to the fence gate to greet us and nose in our pockets for apples whenever we came around, that I wished fervently Ben-dog would return Buck's friendly advances by keeping him company during his own unleashed, outdoor excursions. But my knee-high mutt, ever the smartest member of our household, had quickly sized up the situation: *This* side of the fence suits me very well, thank you, he all but said aloud.

Bigger by far than our cabin had been, with its four bedrooms upstairs and its several downstairs rooms, the farmhouse dated from the turn of the twentieth century, or perhaps a bit earlier. (To many of our friends and family, the extra space seemed ideal for the two or three children who would no doubt soon materialize. But they never did.) The wood floors in particular gave the whole place a distinctly premodern, countrified feel, as most of them weren't made of today's slender, tongue-in-groove boards but rather of broad planks ten inches across, unevenly planed and sanded, punctuated frequently by knots in the pine, and varnished to a warm, pumpkin glow. Here's another way one knew conclusively the house was well past its first youth: in a few places where the old horsehair plaster had crumbled off the thin, vertical strips of wooden lathing to which it had been applied, you could see the wall's inner skeleton—but you found there virtually no upright studs to speak of. No, each wall was built of a solid stack of roughly milled two-by-fours, laid *horizontally* atop one another from floor to ceiling. This stacked-wood construction, we were told, harked back to a time when, in northern New England anyway, wood was still the most abundant and therefore the cheapest resource around, and the best insulator to boot, what with all that cellulose trapping indoor air that was heated by burning still more wood "down cellah" in a furnace designed to do that. (Of modern insulation, then, we had next to none—this in a climate averaging something like fifteen to twenty degrees Fahrenheit for half the year—except for what had been laid down in the attic, and what we added on top of that.) Until we could get around to replacing all the failing plaster with fresh drywall, we sometimes had occasion to knock a wayward board back into place, flush with its stacked fellows above and below. Interesting, indeed.

For me the most appealing feature indoors had to be the big wood cookstove squatting in the center of the large, open kitchen, its gray-enameled oven door stenciled in black ST. LOUIS, MO. The substantial brick chimney against which it sat suggested a degree of division between the kitchen and the dining room, which were otherwise no longer walled off from each other. Though still operable, the stove leaked too much heat from a variety of loose hinges and broken seals for any cooking or baking that called for precise temperatures. But for boiling a kettle, for chasing the ambient chill out of a sleety autumn day when the crows were calling down doom outside the kitchen window, or for keeping my evening reveries company with soft, log-shifting sighs, sizzles, pops, and murmurs: perfect, simply perfect.

When I headed outside, my inner compass needle settled inevitably in the direction of the garden, sited just behind the barn. If there hadn't been nearly enough room for all I dreamed of growing in North Carolina, here I had more than I could easily handle: in went the tomatoes (of multiple varieties), the garlic, the celery, the peppers, the lettuce and spinach, the peas, the green beans, the broccoli, a generous stand of corn, a bed of asparagus, a strawberry patch, blueberry bushes. And still there was room left over, swaths of soil tilled but unplanted, so here came the weeds, the aggressive like of which (burdock, for example) I'd never seen before and haven't seen since. Spreading thick layers of straw all around only just served to choke some of them back. With few trees hard by—unlike my Carolina patch, which had been closely surrounded by woods—a cooling breeze was free to sweep in from the back meadow, and a high blue northern sky always smiled genially upon my summer labors. And upon Buck, reliably posted at the fence so he could snort unsolicited suggestions while shooing flies with his tail. Or so it all seems to me now, in memory. Even Mark—no gardener he—got interested enough in this magical spot one year to plant raspberries. But he grew discouraged when he found they'd need weeding and that a cultivar bought at a greenhouse isn't going to produce berries generously all on its own, the way he knew from years of wilderness backpacking that wild berry bushes invariably will. Not only would he not stoop to weeding (hey, shouldn't everybody and everything, nature included—nature especially—be free to do its thing?), neither would he let me tend those raspberry canes for him. The grass soon swallowed them whole.

Perhaps it's no wonder, with the rest of that big, glorious garden so often crying out to me for some TLC, that my beehive—just one, that first summer—went unattended for weeks at a time. Ergo, a swarm. However, no hive I kept in New England after that experience ever swarmed again. (To my knowledge, anyway—an important caveat, as things can happen when you aren't looking. Although you'd notice if you lost a number of your pigs one afternoon, with bees it's not that simple: you don't open a hive often, and even if you happened to do so right after a swarm, a hive sporting thirty thousand or forty thousand bees doesn't at a glance look much different from one housing half or even a third as many.) The seasons went about their usual, colorful dramas, and I got a little better at timing my hive inspections and knowing when to do what—to add another super or hive story, for example, or to split one colony into two—so as to head off trouble before it started.

Would that I could say the same for my marriage throughout those particular years, but building a happy home proved considerably trickier than building up a thriving apiary, honeybees being easier to fathom by far than *he* ever was. While the hives gradually multiplied and the honey harvests began to yield shelves of glowing jars; while I found myself called upon now and then to wow children and their grandmothers with my glass observation hive at the local farmers' market, or (once) to extricate a colony from within the siding of a house (it didn't work—if you can't get the queen out, you can't get anybody else to come out, either); and while the college allowed me to set up some hives on campus for beekeeping lessons with interested students and faculty—while all this unfolded, all else unraveled. One week your life is more or less intact, and in the next, half of it has ripped loose, absconded, taking with him—what? Not honey, but the very sun, moon, and stars.

"A relationship is a story you construct together and take up residence in," Rebecca Solnit writes, "a story as sheltering as a house." You both move into this narrative with so many hopes, so many giddy plans, so many unspoken certainties, even: that the roof will prove sound, for example, that the foundation will hold fast, that the outer walls and inner fire will ward off interlopers, and darkness, and cold. You want and expect "interesting," thinking yourselves strong enough to face whatever strangeness may lurk within misshapen rooms and cramped little closets. Full of youthful, foolhardy confidence, you even think yourselves able to tackle and set right, over time, the messy effects of building with flawed materials—which you couldn't have helped using in the first place, as that's what both of you brought to the project. If you are very lucky, the years will prove you correct on all these points, or most of them, and you'll both be around much later to muse companionably, with huddled heads and little need for words, over the before-and-after album of photographs.

Mark's departure initially lasted just the few weeks it took me to believe he really meant it, and to decide What Next for myself. Keep the house? Too big, and too much to manage, with its unending maintenance and remodeling issues. (Too much of him still there as well, for good and for bad: I could no longer walk the floors without recalling fondly, painfully, his dark hair crusted over with the sawdust that flew up when we'd refinished them; could also no longer build a fire in the cookstove without hearing the echo of his complaints, for the smell of woodsmoke bothered him; could no longer bear the bright, cheery bathroom, with its white porcelain clawfoot tub and pedestal sink, over which he had erupted in a series of alternating tantrums and pouting spells the summer that a hired carpenter-friend and I refurbished it.) Have him buy me out and shoulder the burden of it? In my weariness over the entire ordeal, which had been a couple of years in the making, that option appealed. After I'd vacated the premises, he'd leave the makeshift loft he had temporarily occupied in town, move back in, and have to pick up from there. Let him live with the ghosts of whatever had died in those half-plastered rooms; I was in a fever to be shut of all of it—especially of him who had long ago been so dear a friend, yet who had come to regard my company as unworthy of his time or energy. Divorce clearly and irrevocably settled upon, he turned suddenly kinder and more solicitous than he'd been in a long while, letting me have anything and everything I wanted—anything except what I wanted most. I made little effort to return the sentiment, heartily wishing him instead frozen plumbing, mouse-mangled wiring, and a tree through the front windows in time for November's snows, as well as no prospective buyers whatsoever, should he decide to sell. (None of it came to pass; he even landed a sale almost as soon as he'd listed the property.) It would be years before I'd fully tire of squeezing the juice from such bitter fruits.

The cozy, restored wing—"Grandma's apartment"—for rent at one end of another old farmhouse some ten miles away became my own next stop, or at least pause. Fortunately, the owner didn't mind my bringing with me Ben and the two cats, Oscar and Ivy, whom Mark and I had also by then acquired. (Buck, having taken to jumping the fence to visit some cows in a field up the road, had long since been removed by his owners to a suitable stable.)

These four-footers were now my chief solace, as in fact they already had been for some time, with their plain animal needs and their uncanny ability to sense and answer mine. And the bees? My hives—just two, at that point—went to campus, to the edge of a tiny orchard the college had recently put in.

A holding pattern of sorts, these next months would be, while I took the time I needed to settle down inside before making any major decisions. It was May when the critters and I tucked ourselves into the new little suite of rooms—planting season, in those parts. But this year there would be no garden, and no bees in residence.

Now someone else, I've no idea who, lingers once in a while in the open door of that lovely barn at the old place, drinking in the mingled fragrances of summers gone by and horses gone elsewhere. And someone else hangs her laundry on the line out back, where a whirlwind of honeybees once showed me in no uncertain terms what they were capable of. And maybe she sings softly to herself, this most recently installed lover of ruins bequeathed by the unknowable past to the present, as she turns, empty basket in hand, to reenter that funky farmhouse Mark and I had set out to renovate, unaware that we ourselves needed rescuing. Maybe she glances up into the apple tree where, chances are, a couple dozen bees murmur among a riot of pale spring blossoms.

A reasonably good way to get that tree out from behind your eyes and the taste of ashes out of your mouth might be to head for other corners of the world. Places like the

Gaspé Peninsula, the northern- and easternmost arm of French-speaking Canada, bordered by the St. Lawrence River on top and the Atlantic along the rounded eastern perimeter. There you can walk a particular trail threading a mist-shrouded forest and emerge at a high, grassy cliff, land's end essentially, to watch and listen to the ocean swell and break, swell and break plaintively upon the continent without surcease. Or the Bay of Fundy, with its roller-coastering tides, and on up to Prince Edward Island's brick-red soil, where enormous Belgian horses splash into the ocean surf up to their chests, dragging big, perforated iron scoops designed to collect valuable seaweeds. When these distractions fail, there are sections of the French Alps, which a friend has agreed to hike with you for a while, as long as you promise to keep her in good coffee, wine, and pastries. Ecuador next, and its lava-pocked Galápagos Islands. The giddy upper reaches of the Peruvian Andes soon after. A short stretch of Australia's Gold Coast and, inland a ways, its bizarre Glass House Mountains. Finally subtropical Japan, for a more extended stay, acquainting university students with American environmental history and roaming, as time permits, ancient cedar groves and ultramodern urban mazes.

But eventually you miss your mom and your dog and you land stateside again, working now with a whole new crop of college students, these with Southern accents. Not in North Carolina this time but near the other end of the Bible Belt—the buckle end, which I place in Texas. Largely overlooked for much of its history and therefore still quite beautiful, Arkansas ("The Natural State") seems a pretty good place to resurrect some old, comforting routines: bee-keeping, gardening, and collecting your mail from just one address for months on end. Your dog doesn't remember you right away, but fortunately your mom does.

For more than two years, then, I did not think much about honeybees. I traveled when school wasn't in session, taught my classes when it was, took up trail running and swimming to tire myself out, grieved the loss of one kind of life and plotted the outlines of another. Upon leaving Maine for good, I had given my active colonies away with no particular regrets: once the decision to move on takes hold, everything familiar loses its luster and you grow impatient to be done with it all, to shake from your sandals the dust of the place where you learned you'd staked much of your life on a lie. And if giving hives away rather than trying to stash them aboard a moving van—alongside mattresses, boxes of books and dishes, and my grandmother's rocking chair—expedites the whole sorry process, so be it. However: I kept my smoker, veil, elbow-length canvas gloves, and hive tool, figuring they'd be called up for service again one day.

And they were.

4

Arkansas Travelers

The bees' religion is posterity.
—JOHN CROMPTON,
A Hive of Bees

Spring in the American South richly deserves all the hosannas that have ever been sung to it, and then some. With lengthening daylight and late-winter rains come the first hints of color, a welcome parting in the drab curtain of browns and grays. Dusky pink japonica petals on mahogany stems, reminiscent of hand-painted Japanese wall hangings; tiny, electric-purple blossoms on misnamed redbud trees; buttery jonquils and, soon after, yellow forsythia. Dewy clumps of lavender wisteria droop heavily from woody vines. Ivory dogwood flowers steal with an Easter quiet onto the scene almost overnight, their graceful, silver-barked limbs holding them up and out as if in stately, decorous offering to some very special guest. Azaleas spread in pastel pink, white, red, and fuchsia across house fronts, churches, and university walkways. Cherry, plum, peach, and pear trees knock themselves out like blooming idiots, tulips spring out of home gardens like candy bursting its cellophane bag; tea roses, spirea, and clematis spill over picket fences; and in the country, wild irises, evening primrose, hairy vetch, and trumpet vines peek out at the brushy edges of fields, and of swamps that have begun to simmer and stew, bubble and croak as if alive, which they are. Across patches of forest floor and many lawns in town, wee little bluets, phlox, spring beauties, and violets work their magic, giving way (too soon, too soon) to bossy swaths of dandelion here, white clover there, deep red clover way over there. Big old catalpa trees with leaves the size of saucers serve up creamy white and yellow blossoms. Fringed mimosa trees ready themselves for the annual show, like so many slender-limbed debutantes with young, salmon-pink complexions. Great masses of pale green foliage coming on quick now, you hear more than see a dozen or so bird species busy mating and nesting—robins, cardinals, bluebirds, juncos, titmice, purple finches, indigo buntings, and the ubiquitous mockingbirds, among others. Fireflies prick the gathering night, and thick, glossy magnolia leaves gleam black under a waxing moon. Evenings quickly warm, bearing upon the breeze a trace of honeysuckle perfume.

If we find all this a heady mix, what must it do to honeybees? It puts them seriously to work is what, making hay while the sun shines. They'll fly any day of the year when the temperature reaches at least the low fifties; in winter these flights are usually "voiding" flights—bathroom trips—but put six or eight such days back-to-back and the bees will decide spring has sprung: time to get cracking.

Which means a good beekeeper will be on the job, too, ensuring the bees have all the room they need to raise vast numbers of young and to store the nectar, water, and pollen (plenty of it, green-dusting everything in sight) that pour into the hive every sunlit hour. But as we've already established, I am not always a good beekeeper. Especially not when I've been out of the bee bid'ness for a couple of years.

After setting up one new hive the preceding summer to get started again, I watched periodically for signs of life at its entrance over the winter, noting with satisfaction in late February that the colony was stepping up its activity, with bees coming and going in increasing numbers. *Good girls, you made it through, and now your queen should be laying again.* My own schedule growing increasingly hectic—as a full-time academic with a heavy teaching load, I'm usually up to my armpits in alligators by March and April—I trusted that the bees could and would look after themselves. And they did, sort of, just not in a way that would leave me a honey harvest. But in a familiar way, nonetheless. Some mistakes bear repeating, I say, so you can be sure to get them right.

A bright early-April day in central Arkansas, say about noon. Hanging wet laundry on the line out back, thinking of little more than whether I'll have enough pins for the job. Ring a bell? My thought exactly, as an odd sound off to the left caught my attention. *What?* Bees, bees, bees. Not swirling around me as they had on that long-ago day in Maine, but already clustered atop the crossbar of one wooden post at the east end of my clothesline, about six feet from the ground. Humming collectively at a kind of low-engine idle.

Oh dear, here we go again. The question is, Am I any more ready for this occasion than I was ten years ago?

Six feet up, just a little ways over my head—that's certainly in my favor. Dropping the laundry basket and hustling into the garage, I scan the junk for some reasonable substitute for the extra hive box I know I don't have, not having gotten around to building any new equipment yet this year. Bicycle, lawn mower, work table, camping paraphernalia, discarded plastic nursery pots, various tools, and heavy-duty extension cords: the usual flotsam of an American household. Nothing that might contain those bees happily overnight, though, not even a cardboard box. Wait. That blue plastic bin over there, with a nice, snug lid: Would that work? I had used it one year to raise earthworms for a vermiculture demonstration during Earth Day celebrations on campus. (The idea of vermiculture is to nurture a little self-contained earthworm community by giving them a bed of newspaper and soil, and feeding them kitchen scraps that might otherwise go into the trash and ultimately to a landfill, where said scraps would not biodegrade for another, oh, bazillion years. Worms, however, will munch the stuff readily and in return provide nutrient-rich "castings"—manure—for use as garden fertilizer.) Eyeing the bin now with a new purpose in mind, I recall with pleasure that a six-by-three-inch section of each side has already been cut out and covered with window screen for ventilation; if I replace one of those screens with light cardboard and cut a bee-sized "door" into it—they'll want badly to be able to come and go, collecting the materials they need to survive—the whole outfit might just do the trick. The bees might find themselves housed comfortably enough to hang around for a few days, till I can get another wooden hive built, painted, and filled with fresh wax foundation.

I head back toward the clothesline to look the situation over again, weighing the possibility of success. How, for example, am I going to get that bin to rest up in the air about five feet, so the bees won't have far to drop when I begin urging them off their post? Must avoid injuring as many bees as possible, most importantly the queen, who should be near the cluster's center. Maybe if I move a stepladder into place just there, underneath—

Which is about as far as I get with the plan. Before my eyes, the cluster dissolves, disperses briefly across a swath of air several feet wide, then gathers itself together once more into a loosely knit, airborne confederation. And moves up, up, and away, over the fence, beyond my neighbor's giant sycamore tree, clean out of sight. *Oh, come back. This really isn't very sporting of you, now, is it? Please come back.* But the scouts in this particular cluster must have done their job well, for they now lead the pack off to a spanking new home.

Heartless little buggers. I turn away, toward the hive they have just abandoned, nestled against the shrubs and crepe myrtle trees lining the northern side of my backyard. A dozen honeybees at the entrance are going about their business unconcerned. I know the colony has already seen to it a new queen will soon be punching in at the time clock, and lots of brood is on the way. Nothing to be done now but wait, to learn whether the remaining bees will build up a strong enough colony this season to overwinter success-fully. Remembering a stack of student essays needing to be marked, I finish hanging the wet laundry and head back in-side.

A little over a week later, and fine, fine weather. Because prepping tomorrow's classes entails reading a couple of chapters in Thoreau, the obvious place to park myself for this work is in a big red Adirondack chair on the back porch, book in one hand and iced tea in the other. The hoary old pecan tree looming high overhead trembles now and then with frenetic squirrel and bird activity, which my chair's orientation allows me to monitor nicely, about once every other paragraph. (Surely Henry won't begrudge it.) Somewhere in the neighborhood someone mows a lawn, putting me in mind of the Mainers I know who are still shoveling wet, late-season snow and channeling, as well as they can, icy runoff away from their house foundations.

And behind my chair, maybe fifteen feet distant, a tell-tale buzzing. I wrench around, disbelieving what I already know for sure is creating that special noise. Indeed, there they are—*atop the eastern crossbar of the clothesline*. Holy moly. Blinking, thoughts racing—*did* that swarm of last week in fact come back? Nah, impossible. Isn't it? By now that crew should be tucked into a hollow tree or some such, who knows where. . . . This must be a different swarm entirely, but where did it come from? Could some-one else in the area be keeping (and losing) bees? I glance over at my one hive on the opposite side of the yard—or did that hive of mine swarm *again*?

Whatever the explanation, I decide quickly not to be had once more if I can help it. Out of the garage come the erstwhile earthworm bin, the stepladder, a piece of light cardboard, a roll of duct tape, and one of a pair of long nylon-web straps I ordinarily use to tie a canoe down to the top of my car. Setting all this aside briefly, glancing again toward the cluster to be sure it's still there on the clothesline—a roast-turkey-size ball of living matter, discernibly smaller than the previous swarm—I dash into the kitchen to put a little water in the kettle to heat up. A few spoonfuls of sugar in a Pyrex measuring cup and some warm water quickly yield a sweet beverage that I intend to spread across the inner floor of the bin, giving the bees a good reason to stay put once they get shoved inside: only honey itself could more readily take a bee's mind off anything else going on around her, fixing her to the spot till all the stuff is lapped up.

But I'm not so bent on success that I'm going to give up any honey (though I have to buy it these days, I always have some around). I mean, there are limits. Sugar water will do.

Back outside, I remove the bin's lid, check that it's clean in there, fit the cardboard into the cut-away opening on one side and tape it in place, and add more tape to the window screen covering the opening on the other side. Several minutes have passed, yet the cluster shows no sign of taking off; but then, in the past they hadn't shown much sign before doing it anyway. A few feet distant, I rig the bin up on the little folding shelf offered by my stepladder—the place for setting down a paint can, NOT FOR STEPPING, as a sticker on it warns—cinching the nylon strap tight around the bulk of the bin and the ladder's vertical legs so the ladder seems to hug the thing snugly against itself. This precaution seems called for by the fact that the bin is longer and wider than a paint can, and would doubtless topple from the shelf once dollops of bees began falling inside and putting weight on the outer edge. Gingerly, I ease the ladder-and-bin structure over to the clothesline, up under the end of the crossbar that the bees have straddled: getting this close with no veil on just yet is a bit unnerving, but the cluster ignores me completely, the pitch of its buzzing not even registering my presence. Very tempting to just stand here and stare. But the window of opportunity, as they say, may be closing on me. Ladder in place, it's time to dress quickly in veil, hat, long-sleeved shirt, and gloves; I'm already in jeans (many styles of white, one-piece bee suits are available for purchase, but I'm cheap). And then to light up the smoker.

You'll sometimes hear it said that the hardest part about beekeeping is maintaining a fire in the smoker. I can vouch for this claim from much personal experience. Smoke has a way of soothing bees, which is why a smoker is among the beekeeper's most important tools. It is usually a metal canister a little taller and bigger around than a tennis-ball can, with a hinged chimney for a lid (reminiscent of the Tin Man's pointy, upside-down-funnel hat in *The Wizard of Oz*) and a bellows attached to one side. Just before opening a hive or otherwise messing with a bunch of honeybees, you put a handful of dry leaves, pine needles, twigs, or scraps of burlap inside the can, light the pile with a match, and then top the fuel off with a few blades of green grass to help your little fire yield smoke through the chimney hole once the lid is closed. If you are lucky, the smoke pours out for several continuous minutes while you direct it toward the hive entrance and up under the hive cover that you are beginning to pry loose with your hive tool. I am almost never so lucky: it seems the fire in my darn smoker always goes out before I've even quite gotten to work, and I have to stop what I'm doing, lift the chimney lid, poke around at the fuel, and fumble with another match, often a pain to pick up out of its box while I am wearing my heavy canvas gloves. I end up yanking a glove off and digging out the match with a bare hand. The smoker lit once more, I pull my glove back on over my shirt sleeve, turn back to the hive, and get a puff or two out of the thing before it dies yet again, on schedule.

But today, lo and behold, either luck or sheer grace is with me for a change: not only does the smoker *stay lit,* it pours forth the thickest, most luxurious smoke I've ever managed to coax out of this contraption. (Could it be the dried magnolia leaves?) Honestly, I can hardly overstate the miracle this is for me, as if Mary herself were making an appearance in thick, pearly-gray plumes that just won't quit. Amazed and immeasurably cheered, I climb up three steps of the ladder, opposite the side holding the plastic bin aloft, the better to reach down toward the cluster from above, and aim the smoke at the bees, using it to direct their movement. As any living thing with half a brain would do, they scuttle quickly away from the hot source of all these choking vapors, the smoker's chimney hole. With my other hand I use a bee brush, a ten-inch wood-handled brush with ultra-fine, ultra-soft bristles that wouldn't hurt a fly, much less a bee, to begin sweeping clotted gobs of bugs into the bin. (They stick somewhat together, like so many hundreds of lumps of gooey, half-melted milk chocolate, thanks to specially designed footpads that allow them to hook onto any surface they wish to stick to—in this case, one another.) Of course, all this disturbance—the smoke, the bee brush, my veiled head and shoulders hovering above—has sent dozens of bees up into the air, flying wildly around as if to cry out, Hey! What gives? Alert and watchful, slow and steady in my movements, I am nevertheless not very worried. A little worried, maybe, which seems to me a healthy outlook to adopt, but not *very* worried. Swarming bees are said to be typically pretty docile. I've heard somewhere a cool explanation for this, to wit: because they have recently filled their bellies with honey, just before departing their original headquarters, they are now too fat to bend themselves into the "C" shape required when they want to sting—like a fat woman who can't bend over to tie her shoes, a honey-engorged bee can't achieve the torque she ordinarily has when she aims to put her stinger, located at the tip of her abdomen, into a victim. I have yet to corroborate this explanation from my reading, but neither have I read anything that contradicts it, so for years I have enjoyed believing it's true. But I wouldn't quote me, if I were you.

The whole effort takes only about twenty minutes. The dumped bees find the sugar water on the floor of the bin and take to it like frat boys to a beer keg; with nearly all the bees inside, and with my fingers figuratively crossed that the queen is among them, I fit the lid down carefully—some bees linger along the top edges, and I'd rather not crush them—and leave the bin right where it is for the nonce, pretty sure the remaining bees flitting about will soon find their way to that little cardboard door. Social beings nearly to a fault, they will want to be with their sisters at any cost: this bin could be a cage, a terrible trap, yet they will file happily inside anyway within the next few hours.

The job done, veil and other equipment put away, I can go back to my seat and my tea on the porch and, turning the chair to give myself a better view of the ladder and bin, settle in for a well-earned rest. Though it went off without a hitch and without a single sting, my palms are damp and the adrenaline still surges: no amount of knowing a swarm isn't usually dangerous will ever take from me the thrill of handling thousands of bees. Staring out at the bin resting just under the clothesline post, thinking how odd it should be that that one spot would draw two swarms to itself, thinking how ridiculously improbable it should be that *all* my swarms seem to involve clotheslines, I decide on a moral to the story: it might be time to invest in an automatic dryer.

Not a week later—the swarm now cozily housed in a real hive, the plastic bin having served its temporary purpose very nicely—while I am out in the yard planting garden seedlings, I hear it. *Again.* That distinctive collective buzz. Not on the clothesline, however, but way overhead, in the boughs of an ash tree. Now I am really stumped: Could these bees *also* have come from the same hive that has already produced two swarms in quick succession? But how can that be—how can one hive give up so many of its numbers, and how does it happen to have so many spare queens?

Clearly, it is high time I read up once more on swarms.

Picture with me for a moment the honeybee's idea of Paradise. The winter has been mild, resulting in relatively few deaths in the colony. The early spring weather has been rainy enough to turn on the pollen and nectar faucets full bore in an endless succession of fresh flowers, but not so wet as to drown everything and shut down the whole jolly show. The colony is disease-free. The queen is in her prime, laying new eggs to beat the band, round the clock; there are more bees hatching out, pupating, and emerging from the nursery than there are aged bees dying from overwork. In short, life is good, real good.

Too good to remain contained within just one or two stacked hive bodies holding ten frames of comb apiece. Eden now begins to feel a bit crowded, and distinctly warmer as well, what with all those thousands of pulsing bodies crawling over and around one another like—well, like a hive brimful of bees. Even constant wing-fanning by large numbers of them brings little relief, especially during the hottest part of each day. At that time, the most sensible thing a house bee can do is head outside and hang from the side of the box, or rest along the bottom board's lip. More than likely, the queen's pheromone isn't reaching all the hive's bees any longer; or maybe she's getting on in life and putting out less juice than before. In either case, there would be less of her controlling scent working its magic on her enormous family. Gradually the same bright idea occurs to several hundred house bees, and so (it would seem) does another: Hey, what say you and me and a few of the gang blow this Popsicle stand sometime soon, make a new start someplace where a girl can breathe for a change? A certain mood steals over the colony, and before they quite know what they are doing or why (again, so it seems), the bees have added to the bottoms of several combs a handful of wax cups, cells large enough to accommodate the raising of new queens. The reigning queen will usually lay fertilized eggs (destined to become female) in these cells, as she ordinarily does in most other cells, but sometimes worker bees don't wait around for her, preferring to move previously laid eggs from other cells into the queen cups. Among the cups, the eggs will be of somewhat different ages, meaning that the new queens will emerge at staggered intervals. These chosen eggs now get the royal treatment— heavy doses of royal jelly—to ensure they develop into queens rather than workers. On the sixteenth day after the first egg was laid, the first virgin queen will break out of her cell, with a little help from some workers chewing away at the wax cap; by then, the old queen and her swarming retinue will already have launched themselves bravely into the world.

As the queen cups are taking shape and taking on royal cargo, the reigning queen picks up on the mood spreading throughout the hive: a change of some import looms. Time to get down to flying trim. She stops eating, stops laying, and keeps moving, apparently to lose weight—and the bees assist her in this project by constantly bullying her (we're talking biting, pushing, and the like) so she won't *want* to pause for breath.

Unless something happens to change the colony's collective mind—a beekeeper destroys the queen cups, for example, or a long spell of rainy weather sets in—the bees will, by the eighth or tenth day since queen rearing began, grow unusually calm and quiet for several days. They are as plump as they'll ever be, having stuffed themselves with honey during this pre-swarm period. Then the big day arrives, though nobody knows it ahead of time, perhaps not even the bees themselves. Around midday, huge numbers of them pour out of the hive, ushering the reigning queen along with them (once in a great while she stubbornly doesn't go; when the swarm realizes as much, they file back into the hive and wait a day or two before trying again). Most of the swarm comprises young, recently emerged worker bees, which makes wonderful sense: this crowd will not be able to replace any of its workers until twenty-one days (the gestation period of a worker bee) after they have chosen a new home, built new comb, and the queen has begun laying again. So the swarm, upon leaving, needs all the longevity it can muster, which it achieves by taking with it the youngest and strongest.

Meanwhile, back at honeybee HQ, plenty of brood of varying ages is on hand to begin replacing, a little at a time, the bees that have absconded, as well as the oldest, soon-to-be-history bees that remained behind. And those developing queens tucked away in their cups, what of them? Within a week or so of the first or "prime" swarm's departure, the oldest of the virgin queens makes her debut in the hive. Not quietly: she comes on the scene making a high-pitched racket—"piping"—and emitting as well her own pheromone, her own chemical scent. By these two means she's essentially telling the colony, "Listen up, everybody. Everything's fine; I'm in charge now." Her piping causes all the workers nearby to freeze right where they are, for as long as she keeps up the noise. Unless she, too, flies the nest soon with her own passel of bees—an "afterswarm"—the colony will usually accept her as their new lady and liege, and neglect to come to the aid of other queens who, over the next few days, will begin piping to be let out. Which in turn means that those developing queens, potential pretenders to the crown, are essentially calling out their locations to their own murderess, the firstborn queen. She moves swiftly, deliberately toward them. Chewing a tiny hole in one of the wax cups, she inserts a deadly stinger. Equipped though she is with such elegant weaponry, just as the workers are, a queen uses her stinger only on other queens, usually in situations like this. But unlike a worker bee, a queen can sting and live to tell about it—and to sting again. The deed done at the first cup, then, she goes looking for her next victim. If any other queen emerges before the first can find her, they fight it out, until one of them stands victorious over the dying body of the other.

Unless she, too, flies the nest soon. If the springtime hive is really chock-full of brood and still generously populated by mature bees even in the wake of a prime swarm, an afterswarm is likely. As many as four afterswarms may occur over the course of about a month, each one attended by a newly emerged virgin queen. (A hive overtaken by the swarm fever will keep up a ready supply of developing queens.) How it happens that these successive swarms may be drawn to the same clothesline post is, I suppose, anyone's guess.

In early May I had to travel for a few days, and returned to hear that there had been a bit of buzz downtown in my absence. Police, Animal Control officers, yellow crime-scene tape, local news media, alarmed shopkeepers and passersby—you get the picture: a swarm of honeybees had clustered on a telephone pole on Oak Street. You and I both know now what the good citizens of Conway didn't know, and what I didn't know that far-off day in Maine, when I witnessed my first swarm: this cluster had simply paused for a spell to allow its scouts to do their thing, to find a new nesting site. Presumably its just-vacated home was close by. Since my honeybees and I live just a few blocks away . . . well, if you're thinking what I'm thinking, then I'm thinking we're both right. That incredible first hive of mine had very likely sent out a fourth swarm. As I was nowhere to be found that momentous day, some other local beekeeper was summoned by the authorities to come to Oak Street and save Western civilization, which he was naturally happy to do: free livestock, bully for him.

Thus ended a little adventure, a pleasant Saturday afternoon out on the town, launched by that particular pack of yearning, churning, restless bees. Until next time.

5

Of Origins and Metamorphoses

Following signs and instances like these,
Some testify that bees possess a share
Of the World-Spirit and the Mind Divine.
For God, they say, is immanent in all,
Land, sea and sky's immensity; from Him
All flocks and herds, wild nature and mankind,
Each at their birth, draw down their ghostly lives;
Then unto the same are rendered back
At dissolution, nor give room for death,
But float up living to the starry heights,
And duly there assume the astral form.

—VIRGIL, BOOK IV,
Georgics (translated from the Latin by T. F. Royds)

I.

In generous moods, I'm not much inclined to begrudge my swarming bees their wanderlust, their urge to seek out greener pastures and some cozy new hole in the wall. I'm rather given to pulling up stakes now and then myself, and for similar reasons—to find and make a home, someplace where the flowers bloom small and sweet and all over creation. Trouble is, even when you find such blessed fields, so do the frosts, eventually. Every place, every person, every darn *thing* in nature (and everything derives ultimately from nature) is shot through with a crack of some kind, as Emerson put it, a flaw or a pitfall, one or more imperfections that stir in us every response from mere annoyance to hair-tearing agony. Thanks largely perhaps to the Romantic poets, the internal combustion engine, electricity, and penicillin, many of us seem to have forgotten that nature, generally speaking, is not altogether on our side—that the nature of nature is frequently to be contrary, to resist what we humans would have it be, or what we'd have it do. In other words, to be less than perfect or to behave less than perfectly, as we would like to define that notion. You go to stake a tent, and there seems always to be a rock beneath what appeared to be pure soil; you put up a house, and a tornado flattens it; you try your hand at some important endeavor for days and nights on end, but your body betrays you with its need for sleep; you mean to live forever, but your body betrays you utterly. The odd fact in all this may be not that nature seems poorly calibrated to satisfy human longing, every which way we turn, but rather that we constantly expect it to be otherwise.

No wonder we tell ourselves, in certain circles, a story about a fallen world, a world stained through and through by the wrongdoing of the only two people who ever got to see it in its original, perfect glory, and who therefore knew a more profound loss than the rest of us can imagine. Who among us would trade his regrets over his own youthful folly for theirs? In other circles, the story of original perfection and subsequent decline is not about a garden but about a cave, not about fruit but about fire and sunlight, not about sin but about the frailty of human understanding. In this version, the story of Plato's cave, everything we encounter in life is said to be like a shadow cast by firelight on a cave wall, an imperfect approximation of an original, ideal Form corresponding to and informing that thing, an ideal that necessarily exists outside of time, beyond the cave entrance in the sunlight of pure Truth, outside the ruinous forces of change. In our world, plump little babies grow into brittle old men with hair curling out of their ears, and splendid marble columns weather away, crumbling to nothing. But among the Forms, human souls both preexist their incarnation as babies and outlast their elderly shells; the Form "marble column" spends eternity as a perfectly lovely marble column.

Plato's Greek forebears told one another of an original, golden age when the Olympic gods created humankind, people who, as the poet Hesiod says in his *Works and Days*, "lived as if they were gods, / their hearts free from all sorrow, / by themselves, and without hard work or pain; no miserable / old age came their way; their hands, their feet, did not alter." Though mortal, these first human beings died painlessly, as if merely falling asleep. "All goods / were theirs" back in that perfect day, and "The fruitful grainland / yielded its harvest to them / of its own accord." Later generations were considerably worse off, partly because Zeus chose to afflict them with a comely but unscrupulous woman named Pandora, who bore a jar full of troubles—injustice, poverty, betrayal, you name it—that she loosed upon the world simply by lifting the lid. This, to Hesiod, is why nature is so uncomfortable and uncooperative, for now

> the earth is full of evil things,
> and the sea is full of them;
> there are sicknesses that come to men by day,
> while in the night
> moving of themselves they haunt us,
> bringing sorrow to mortals,
> and silently, for Zeus of the counsels
> took the voice out of them.

Only one spirit—that of Hope—remained in the jar that Pandora opened.

As different as all these narratives are, what interests me at the moment is their similarities: this world, earth, is depicted as Less Than, a place where human life is unendingly vulnerable. None of them answers the yearning for a place of rest in this life we wake to every day, a place *here* of complete peace of mind and heart; rather, all of them make plain that such rest isn't going to happen. But two of them, the Christian and the Platonic stories, insist that such a world not only once was but will be again, elsewhere and elsewhen. And the mere fact that we have such stories seems to explain why a body would ache for some flawless dream of an existence in the first place: if I look all around but see no specimen of the perfect rose or the perfect orange or the perfect human life, it must be because I have some idea of "the perfect" against which I am measuring all the roses, oranges, and human circumstances of my acquaintance. Which idea, Lord knows, must have come from somewhere.

Then there's another, very different story of the world's original condition we in the West have come to tell ourselves, though only very recently: the story of the "big bang," followed much later by the generation and evolution of living beings by natural selection. Compared to the older stories, this one is kind of weird for where it places perfection—not way back in the oldest past, which it suggests was rather barren of creature comforts (just a black void, and eventually a big rocky planet swathed in rain clouds), but somewhere far ahead in the future. This story, especially the part concerning evolution, essentially lets go of the notion of perfection altogether, thinking instead in terms of constant *improvability*, constant change, perfection being an ever receding, unreachable horizon. This horizon lies not just out there but also *up* there, for evolution has come to be equated (in the popular mind, anyway) with progress, with upward mobility, perhaps the key idea to come out of the Enlightenment. Dealing though it does in unthinkably long reaches of time, evolution is curiously not much preoccupied with the past, which is another way of saying it's got very little use for memories. Especially those concerned with old mistakes: working by trial and error, evolution unceremoniously consigns errors—features of physiology or behavior that prove to have no survival value—to oblivion. I don't know, but I wonder: Could that be one reason not a lot of people are crazy about it, about evolution? I mean, it's a pretty cold fish (so to speak) to hand someone who's come to know a thing or two about mistakes, and about the shortcomings and faults that lie not in our stars, and not just in nature, but in ourselves. Compared especially to the Judeo-Christian origin story, evolution has so little to say to us about memories, especially about how to live with—or atone for—the bad and the sad ones.

The evolution narrative differs from earlier stories in another interesting way, by emphasizing to a far greater extent that human vulnerability is not *only* human; many of the challenges and ills that our flesh is heir to afflict other beings as well, at some time or other. (Except maybe bee sting; other animals have more hair and hide than we do with which to fend it off.) Bobcats and boll weevils, bees and beekeepers: somehow we all have to do our best to grow up and make a living—indeed, make a life—before living itself is done. Together, evolution and big-bang theory present the message that we humans, too, are creatures, made of the same carbon molecules that leaped out of the stardust to earth and set about building all life-forms. This idea may rob us of some flattering notions about human uniqueness, but in return it reassures us we are not altogether alone.

Which came first, the flower or the bee? To biologists, the question is less riddlesome than it initially seems. The flower preceded the bee by some twenty million years, give or take, putting other critters to work on its behalf well before the honeybee was even a gleam in its daddy's big, compound eye. And just who was Daddy? A wasp of some kind, a reformed carnivore that had seen the light and gone vegetarian. That is, somewhere in the hinterlands of Gondwana, the ancient continent that once joined Africa to parts of Europe, a waspy ancestor of the honeybee had relinquished its gustatory preference for other insects and spiders, evolving instead both a taste for plant juices and pollen, and the mouthparts to eat them with. Most important to the flowers was another development in bees that we might call the werewolf phenomenon: they grew hairy. To a flower, insect hair is prime pollen collection-and-distribution equipment, as sticky pollen grains readily snag on it and hitch a ride. With their legs and while in flight, the bees clean at least some of that pollen off themselves and tuck it into the longer hairs of their two hind legs, hairs which curl around to form "corbiculae"—science lingo for shopping baskets—so as to make the trip back to the hive with two full loads of protein-rich food.

The arrival of bees in the world approximately one hundred million years ago had tremendous implications for flowering plants, for despite the latter's greater age, not until the vegetarian bees came along did angiosperms exhibit anywhere near the vast numbers or mind-blowing variety that exists today. "Flowering plants" includes, of course, dozens, if not hundreds, of tree species. All that greenery spilling over the planet throughout the millennia in turn made a big difference in much else that we now take for granted. Try to picture it: trillions of trees and other plants proliferating through the endless roll of the seasons, eon upon eon, across all the continents and nearly as far as the polar ice caps. In that Discovery Channel of the mind, watch whole forests of plants flourish in summer, die back in winter, watch the trees leaf out in one season and shed their leaves the next, watch them grow tall for a century or more before crashing to the earth, there to spend another century moldering away. Throw in the occasional monsoon, volcanic eruption, and cataclysmic earthquake. Watch all this growth, death, decay, and new growth, and then whisper to yourself, reverently if you feel so moved: Soil. Microbes, earthworms, termites. Ants, anteaters, lizards, voles, owls, and all the beings that eat anteaters and lizards, voles and owls. Grass. Petroleum, coal, diamonds. Relatively moist, breathable air, and large bands of temperate climate swaddling the globe, thanks to the regulatory power of plant life over its immediate environs. Now think again of the pollinators, about one thousand species of which are some type of bee, and consider anew the part they've played in clothing our planet thus magnificently, in bathing it with precious oils and studding it with jewels.

Among bees, those species that collect nectar far outnumber the ones that both collect and store it (in the form of honey) for future use. It is this habit of setting aside a spoil-proof surplus that has made the latter important to humans since our own earliest days—since we were more hominid than human, in fact. For most of our history, no other sweetener was available to us; yet from the start the human animal has had a terrific sweet tooth, evolved in tandem with his fruit-heavy diet. Much like bears, ratels (a type of badger found in parts of Africa and Asia), and certain martens, weasels, and polecats, early hunting-and-gathering peoples sought honeybee nests most often when they could be expected to be full of honey: late summer and early autumn, in the temperate regions. And they helped themselves to much else besides: larvae and wax comb are perfectly edible (as are adult bees, though their consumption appears to have occurred much less frequently), and both are still enjoyed in several parts of the world to this day.

For many thousands of years, this honey hunting preceded beekeeping as such. As human life began to settle down somewhat—the rise of agriculture around ten thousand years ago meant fields in need of supervision, which encouraged sedentary habitation—honeybee colonies began to be collected from the wild, live and intact, often by cutting away the hollowed-out section of a tree trunk in which bees had nested and bringing it close to home for deliberate tending. By the time Europeans had added beekeeping to their farm work, *Apis mellifera* had become their species of choice simply because it was the one most widely available in that part of the world, having come up from Africa eons before through the Mediterranean territories. Within this species there are several races, so called because of regionally distinct traits that emerge when one species spreads out over a vast area. *Apis mellifera ligustica* has been the most important in the West in modern times. More casually known as Italians, these bees share with their human counterparts of southern Europe a reputation for being friendly and easygoing, and for raising large families. That is, they are not so quick to sting as other honeybees, preferring to concentrate on building up their hive numbers so as to have that many more hands available for gathering pollen and nectar. A denser hive population also means a better chance of overwintering successfully, which in turn gives them a big advantage, come spring, over other pollen and nectar collectors, most of whom are just ambling into the starting blocks by the time the honeybees have completed a half dozen laps. And this, to a beekeeper, eventually means surplus honey for the taking. Other races are preferred by some beekeepers for various traits they offer, such as the Carniolan (originally from Austria, it withstands northern winters fairly well) and the Russian (more zealously hygienic in its housekeeping, it may ward off disease better than other races).

In just the last thirty years in the United States, the African race *A. m. scutellata* (sometimes classified as *A. m. adansonii*) gained celebrity even among those who otherwise scarcely give honeybees a passing thought. This is the so-called killer bee that was brought from Africa to Brazil in the 1950s and accidentally released there. Two of this bug's traits, its highly aggressive nature and its habit of swarming frequently, have led it to wreak havoc among apiaries as it has spread from South America up through Central America and Southern California, and as far east as Texas. For now, its northern progress appears to be slowing, and perhaps halting altogether, at the edges of regions that receive fairly significant annual rainfall; having evolved in Africa's driest parts, this character doesn't much like getting wet. "Killer" is really too harsh a term for this bee, feeding imaginations with the stuff of sensational cinema, so the preferred term among bee people is Africanized honeybee, or AHB. The real problem isn't that AHB moves murderously through the land in search of people and livestock (it doesn't), but that it gradually supplants other races of *A. mellifera* by outcompeting their drones reproductively, thereby altering the nature of one's apiary with offspring exhibiting AHB's greater aggressiveness and tendency to abscond, both of which work against a beekeeper's plans. If you hope to get some honey or wax from your colony, you need a bee that's not going to sic its cavalry on you as you approach the hive, and one that's not going to skip out on you several times a year. You need something much closer to that gentle, hardworking, homebody Italian. Thus you'd really rather your Italian queen exercise some judgment in her choice of boyfriends, opting for the familiar, good-natured locals over the exotic bullies that may have recently rolled into town. That way she's more likely to generate hordes of productive honeybee citizens with positive attitudes, as opposed to a line of thugs and runaways.

How the queen actually goes about mating and subsequently filling the nursery is a subject to which we will want to address ourselves in due course. But before we get to all the juicy honeybee sex (and trust me, it's wild stuff), this seems a good place at which to pause and call attention once more to what we've got on our hands: an origin story, both for the honeybee and, implied in very broad outline, for all other life-forms as well, including the human being. It's the story told by twenty-first-century biology, and though it may be generally familiar to all of us and thoroughly accepted by quite a lot of us, it's not one we would have comfortably entertained had we been born just a couple centuries earlier. Indeed, many do not buy it now—another subject to be addressed momentarily. As origin stories go among peoples throughout the world, the evolution narrative is quite the sassy young upstart, still very new on the scene but willing to brook no competition from other such narratives, no matter how hoary or venerable. It has excellent reasons for considering itself the once-and-for-all truth about every living being's genealogical past (though it's still pretty vague on the origin of life itself), and for deeming all the other stories that came before "myth" or "lore," beginning with the fact that the latter usually involve supernatural forces, whereas the story told by science never does, natural forces and events being really so much easier to detect and measure empirically. But one generation's lore is its great-great-great-great-great-grandfather's truth. What's more, despite all that science can tell us about the world—and this is a very great deal, to be sure—its methods necessarily leave out of bounds certain realms of inquiry, realms legitimated by the simple fact that human beings have entered them time and again, and probably always will. Poetry, for example, and storytelling of all kinds, where "facts" and material explanations may be in short supply but where meaning of an entirely different order may nevertheless reside.

Out of respect for our ancestors, then, and out of interest in whatever meaning they glimpsed by the means they had at their disposal, a moment's consideration of earlier origin stories for at least the honeybee seems called for, if the hardcore evolutionists among you will kindly indulge me.

The ancients of the Western world believed that honeybees emerged from the rotting flesh of an ox killed according to a specific protocol, a grim one involving a terrible beating in a small room with four windows facing the cardinal directions. The idea is thought to have originated in Egypt, which may explain why Apis—the name for a sacred bull of that country—came to mean "bee" in Latin, and eventually to designate the genus. (The species name for the honeybee, *mellifera*, means "honey producing"; in ancient Greece, *melissa* denoted honey, and Melissa was also the name of a Delphic priestess.)

As the classical Roman poet Virgil told of the bee's origins in the fourth poem of his *Georgics,* however, Egyptian notions weren't in the mix. Rather, the honeybee–ox connection derived from the Greek myth of Aristeus, god of beekeeping, who at one point lost all his bees to disease and was at pains to understand why, and to find out how he could recover or replace them. The answer Aristeus arrived at to his first question concerned the ignominious role he had played in ruining the happiness of Eurydice and her lover, Orpheus. " 'Vengeance divine pursues thee,' " Virgil imagines Aristeus being told, for his having chased Eurydice along a river, where she was fatally struck by a serpent hiding in the grass. Inconsolable over the loss of his bride, Orpheus played upon his lyre song after exquisitely mournful song, inadvertently stirring all the foregone dead to bewildered, ghostly attention. His grief was so great, so poignant, as to actually win for him what anyone in a similar circumstance would gladly give a decade of his own life to have: a chance to mend the break in his heart, to undo the past, to retrieve Eurydice from Tartarus and take her home. On condition: that he himself descend into the underworld to fetch her, that he not speak to her, that he go before her as they departed the halls of the dead, and that he not once look back. Eagerly Orpheus went for her, then started to retrace his steps while she followed. They had nearly made it out, they were virtually " 'neath the very shores of light," as Virgil says, when "Alas for memory and for mind's control! / [He] looked back on his Eurydice." Only to see her melt into shadow as he lost her a second time, this one terribly final. The Polish poet Czesław Miłosz pictures Orpheus at this point falling senseless to the earth amid "a fragrant scent of herbs, [and] the low humming of bees."

From this distance it wouldn't quite seem punishment enough that Aristeus should only lose his bees for attempting rape and thereby putting Eurydice in harm's way, until we recall that Aristeus was the *god* of beekeeping: without his hives, he was nothing, a washout, a total zero. (Or maybe not so total: he was also the god of cheesemaking.) What to do? "Hold out thy gifts / And sue for peace and pardon," Virgil says he was advised. Instructed to sacrifice four bulls and four heifers, and to leave their carcasses for nine days, Aristeus does as he is told and returns to find "A wondrous prodigy: within the kine, / Throughout the molten flesh, are buzzing bees; / From bursten ribs they pour, and trail in clouds / Endless, and now upon a tree-top swarm, / And hang a cluster from the drooping boughs." This is the happy note upon which Virgil ends his *Georgics*: forgiveness sought, forgiveness granted, error atoned for, resurrection of a sort made real. And bees aplenty to keep the world in honey and wax, sweetness and light.

One character in the story deserves special mention: Proteus, one of the minor ocean gods and a seer who "knoweth all, / What was and is and what is soon to be," but who also does not give up his secrets to just anyone for the asking. He it is whom Aristeus must find and compel to speak, if he would understand why he lost his bees. Aristeus' mother, Cyrene, warns him that he will have to steal up to Proteus, grab him and hold tight while the seer goes violently through a series of shapes intended to scare off his assailant:

> For he will suddenly
> Turn into bristled boar or tigress dire,
> Scaled dragon or a tawny lioness,
> Or crackle sharply into flame, and so
> Elude thy bonds, or into water glide
> And thinly ooze away.

Mom is always right, of course, so throughout this ordeal our hero hangs on, until Proteus calms down, resumes his own shape, and gives up what he knows—that angry, grief-addled Orpheus has cursed Aristeus with a form of loss as close to his own as he, Orpheus, can manage.

This and many other Greek myths about the origins of things lost credibility in the minds of educated elites with the rise, in the fifth and sixth centuries B.C.E., of rational philosophy à la the pre-Socratic thinkers, Socrates himself, and Plato, the fellow who came up with the cave analogy. Eventually Platonic idealism (his notion of the perfect Forms) would also lose at least some ground to other notions, though not before significant parts of it were absorbed by early Christianity—most important, the idea of everlasting human souls (this wasn't in the Jewish theology that gave rise to the new religion until at least the second century C.E.; rather, Judaism taught that immortality is achieved through one's posterity). And there was Plato's student Aristotle, a proto-scientist in his preference for close observation of nature as a means of understanding the physical world. He wrote a great deal about honeybees, more than anyone before him, as far as we know. If he got a few things wrong about them in his *Historia animalium* — such as the idea that honeybee young are gathered by workers from olive-tree flowers and placed in the comb to pupate—he also got some things right, such as the facts that wax cells for raising drones are larger than those made for workers, and that bees live off their honey stores through the winter. Some of Aristotle's quainter notions would hang on uncorrected for many hundreds of years: for instance, that the colony's ruler is a king bee, and that honey itself falls like dew from the sky.

Centuries later, Christianity and candles having come along and all the witches having been hung (this is Thoreau talking), Westerners completely forsook ancient beliefs that bees come from olive-tree blossoms or from dead oxen in favor of another: God had created them on one of those

illustrious days of the world's first week of existence, probably the fifth day, when the Bible says God created the
winged creatures. Indeed, the opening book conveniently
hinted at the Deity's own hand in creating *everything* during that extraordinary week—hence the title "Genesis."
Hence also the long and fiercely held idea of immutable
species: every being that lives, flies, crawls, walks, or swims
looks and behaves today exactly as it did at the dawn of
the world, when God gave form to what had been chaos,
making all the crucial distinctions—between light and
dark, day and night, heaven and earth, land and sea, between insects and amphibians, goats and sheep, between
male and female. Every being had its separate place in the
scheme of things, as God had seen fit to assign, and the
scheme was hierarchical, a "great chain of being," with
lowly creatures like centipedes near the bottom and humankind near the top, in the neighborhood of the angels. If
sometimes something seemed a bit out of kilter in the natural order—if a baby was born with both male and female
genitalia, for example—well, it just went to show that
God's just punishment for Adam and Eve's sin was still at
work in the world, or, alternatively, that Satan could (as
the priests frequently averred) visit his evil at any time
upon the unsuspecting, the unready, or the unholy. Devia-
tions from the norm came in many different guises, but
they were rare enough to pose no threat to the basic notion
of immutable species. It was a completely satisfactory and
serviceable theory—or rather, not a "theory" at all but the
Truth, God-given and therefore sacred, unassailable. Immutable, one is tempted to say.

So it seemed for the longest time, until the annoying appearance over the eighteenth and nineteenth centuries of several unorthodox thinkers with various bees in their bonnets. Nagging ideas about time, change, plant and animal physiology, the age of the earth, the Bible's textual origins in human history and culture, and the very different stories of creation to be found among peoples of the world so unfortunate as to have been born somewhere other than Europe.

Right-thinking Western intellectuals found the exotic creation stories fairly easy to dismiss. These were preposterous notions, such as the Chinese idea that the world had begun when chaos separated into the two parts of a hen's egg, with the lighter and heavier parts, respectively thought of as yang and yin, serving as male and female essences that would infuse all things to come. The egg also produced a giant named Pangu, who grew to be as big as the whole world before he died; his decomposing body gave rise to mountains, rivers, precious metals, and gems. Or there was the Algonquin story of Earth Mother's two sons, Glooskap (the wise, creative one) and Malsum (the selfish, destructive brute), who fashioned between them all that was good and horrible in the world—edible plants and animals on the one hand, snakes and vermin on the other. These and all the rest of the lot—stories brought to European ears by a couple of centuries of global exploration, itself the result of many years' worth of improvements in navigation and mapmaking—need not, it was thought, disturb modern European halls of learning or worship overmuch: they were just the superstitions of pagans who ate funny things and, in some cases, ran around wearing hardly a stitch. And anyway those myths wouldn't hang on in their native regions much longer; dedicated (not to mention disease-ridden) conquistadors and missionaries would see to that.

But other difficulties remained to afflict many who had taken in with mother's milk the idea of immutable species: fossil remnants of strange creatures not mentioned in the Bible and no longer anywhere to be seen; striking similarities between such physiological structures as a dolphin's flipper and a bird's wing, though dolphins and birds seemed to fall in very different places on nature's ladder; developmental changes experienced by individual animals, such as a frog's emergence out of a tadpole; changes that people could effect in some plant and animal species by selective breeding techniques; and the radical idea, put forth by Charles Lyell in his *Principles of Geology*, published in 1830, that the earth was much, much older than the few thousand years implied by the Bible—which, if true, would allow for slow, gradual changes in species over the course of generations. Then, too, there was the work of several German biblical scholars in what was called the higher criticism: historical research that strongly suggested there had once been more parts to the Scriptures than the venerated King James translation encompassed, and that many of the Bible's teachings reflected cultural assumptions and social mores that had obtained among the Hebrews— among ordinary human beings, in other words—two thousand years before. All these and other disturbing developments slowly began the Holy Book's undoing as the thinking man and woman's source of truth about the world. Including its physical origins, and the supposed immutability of species. Even the origin of humanity itself.

Seen in a certain light, the Bible's version of creaturely origins began to look distressingly not much less fanciful than that of the Algonquins or Chinese, especially after Charles Darwin established in the mid–nineteenth century a rational, empirically sound basis for an alternative line of thought—evolution—that had been gaining strong intellectual ground for many decades. Not that the Genesis story (as a literal account of how species came to be) has been going down ever since without a spirited fight, a long and ugly one that still rages, particularly among members of some public school boards. But evolutionary theory has had its own conquistadors and missionaries, and the weapons of choice in *this* battle of origin stories have been university degrees in biology, government funding for research, peer review of journal articles, and the like. Serious armaments, meaning anyone who would pursue a career in science had best put any creationism he may harbor behind him.

Long before Darwin published his landmark *Origin of Species* in 1859—long before he was even born, actually: his own grandfather published a book on the subject—the fact that evolution happens was pretty well established in the minds of natural philosophers, as scientists were then called. What they didn't have, and what Darwin provided, was a convincing explanation of *how* it happens. This is the source of Darwin's fame (or infamy, depending on your politics), not as author of the idea of evolution, but as interpreter of the story's basic plot. With no knowledge of chromosomes or genes (that knowledge wouldn't come along for another half century), he intuited that heredity from parent to offspring is the primary mechanism of evolution, augmented by environmental pressures such as available food supply. That is, only those animals and plants with the "fitness" to make the most of their environments would live to reproduce, and in reproducing they would pass on to their offspring the traits that made for fitness. Less fit creatures would die, usually before reaching reproductive maturity, so whatever traits had held them back would die with them. Working together, these two aspects of natural selection would yield generations of critters able to exploit their environments to the utmost. But "environments"—a rather sterile word for habitats—do not stand still. As they change, both plants and animals have to change with them in order to survive as species. Over very long stretches of geological time, these adaptations occasionally give rise to new species entirely (the basic definition of "species" being the ability of its members to produce fertile offspring), sometimes because the random appearance of a genetic mutation proves helpful to survival in one group and thus makes its development take a new turn, while the cousins continue developing along the original path. Or in other cases, because a relatively sudden environmental change separates members of a species so completely as to give rise to new paths of development in each population, as when a landmass breaks up into a handful of islands and permanently separates the plants and animals left alive upon them after the split.

Natural selection, according to this account, is thus the author of species—of speciation itself, and of all the world's grand diversity.

And look, Mom, no hands in all of this: no hand of God required—not even in the slow rise, out of the mists of prehistory and from simian ancestors, of a species to be called *Homo sapiens*.

As I write, the First Church of the Nazarene in Conway, Arkansas, is gathering across the street from my house for Sunday services. I'm not altogether sure of their theology, but I can guess that many if not all of the congregation find science's story for plant and animal origins—and certainly for that of the human being—anathema. They are not alone: in twenty-first-century America, one of the world's most educated societies, more citizens than not continue to prefer the Genesis story, to the exasperation of scientists and most other intellectuals as well. Not every creationist takes everything in Genesis literally; many choose, for example, to view its seven "days" as symbolic of geologic eras. But many certainly do read the entirety literally, especially the fundamentalists holding fast to the idea that all of the Bible is God's word, plain and simple, as breathed into the ears of specially chosen Jewish and Christian scribes. Besides its challenge to this biblical literalism, evolution has upset so many Christians for several additional reasons, according to the religion-and-science scholar Ian Barbour: it places the human being squarely among the animals, rather than in a lofty, separate sphere reserved for the quasi-divine, and it implies, in certain interpretations, endorsement of a brutally competitive social ethos in which concern for and assistance to the weak among us (a major Christian value) would work seriously against the "progress" of our own species as nature appears to define it.

And of course, not least among the creationists' problems with science's narrative is its removal of a Heavenly father, to say nothing of Heaven itself, from the picture. As if all the astounding order and variety and inexpressible magnificence of the whole bean-green-and-blue planet can be explained by blind natural law operating randomly upon matter, with no special agenda or game plan, and no special reason or power to endow the human being with a soul, much less any interest whatsoever in guiding the trajectory of a particular person's one small, precious, irreplaceable life, or any interest in whisking her off after death to a place where the livin' is easy—a place she imagines she can finally call home. When science's philosophical materialism—its assertion that physical matter is all there is, and all *we* are—sets out to conquer all forms of idealism, it takes no prisoners.

Fortunate Algonquins, with their one simple story that seemed, to them, to speak both physical and metaphysical truth. We who inherited the European West's traditions have it so much less easy, trying to find some way to live with either a story that outrages sense (how could woman have possibly been created from one guy's rib?) or one that outrages spirit: careful though it may be for a time of the type (the species), as Tennyson remarked, natural law cares not a whit for the individual. That would be you, Dear Reader, and that would be me.

II.

Well. Might not hurt to lighten up right about now. I promised to deliver some hot insect hanky-panky, so okay: it's time you send the little ones out of the room. Several pages back we had a virgin queen emerging from her cocoon and roaming across the comb to look for other pupating queens to dispatch with her stinger, exquisitely adapted over the millennia to serve her murderous purpose. Rivals duly dealt with, now what?

She spends a few days just more or less hanging out in the hive, getting used to her digs and her loyal subjects and letting them get used to her while her body continues to mature. Then she aims for the light—the hive entrance at its bottom board—and flexes her wing muscles, contemplating (we might imagine) the wide world beyond her front door. She still has her slender, girlish figure, and at this point in her maidenhood she knows exactly what to do with it: head for the aerial hangouts frequented by young honeybee studs. Virginity, to a fresh honeybee queen, can't be lost quickly enough.

Having made a few short orientation flights right around the hive to get her bearings—on the landing board, some workers linger, lift their abdomens, and release a special pheromone of their own into the vicinity, to help her find her way back—the queen finally takes to the air on what's called her nuptial flight, which actually may amount to several flights over the course of several days. During this time she will fly anywhere between one and five miles

from her hive, and she'll mate with drones who have typically come from several different nests lying between one
and two miles apart from hers. She heads up, up, and
away, in search of drone-congregation areas: patches of air
some thirty to ninety feet high, places where the boys can
be found cruising. How the queen locates such areas, she
who has never been abroad before now, is remarkable in
itself. But the wonder of it all deepens: How is it that the
drones know where to find these places? It's not as if
they've had older brothers leading them to these spots,
which remain roughly the same from year to year, because
there's no such thing as honeybee brothers older by more
than a few days or weeks at most; all have been born in this
new, spring season—yet they've headed for the same con-
gregating areas that earlier generations of drones had used
in their day.

However it happens, the boys are in the vicinity when
our virgin queen passes through, and, sensing her arrival,
they launch a mad chase. Hundreds, sometimes thousands,
will take off after her at once, the fastest in the lead, forming a "drone comet"—a term coined by sober science—
reminiscent of a swarm. And although the Preacher cautions
us that the race is not always to the swift, in honeybee
courtship it most certainly is. The first fellow to catch up to
the queen is the first to have her.

The mating act is the drone's great moment. Until now
he's done little more than loiter back at the hive, chowing
down on honey and grooming himself—waiting, like any
adolescent, to grow up so he can run the airy streets in
search of girls. (Of course, within the hive he's utterly sur-

rounded by them, but jeez, these are his *sisters,* not the sort of girls he has in mind.) His prodigious organ—an "endophallus"—is ordinarily tucked up discreetly within his abdomen; the drone on a mating chase eagerly deploys it. Even beyond the presumed thrill and obvious significance for the hive's future, this is the drone's great moment for the sheer acrobatics involved: a trapeze artist lunging in midair for his fast-flying partner, he mounts the queen from behind and within a blinding second is catapulted into a backflip by the force of his own ejaculation. The physical force of it takes an immediate toll, tearing away the drone's genitals and part of his abdomen, so that he falls to the ground mortally wounded. Poets fond of connecting sex with death cannot tell a drone honeybee anything he doesn't already know.

But the queen flies carelessly on, oblivious even to the plug of tissue that her lover has left hanging out of her sting chamber (the sting itself rests conveniently off to one side of the opening). This plug or "mating sign" is easily pushed away by the next drone to catch up with her, and so it goes through several lovers, easily as many as fifteen or twenty over several days' time, until her two oviducts are replete with semen. Then she'll return to the hive a confirmed matron and not leave it again, unless a swarm persuades her otherwise. A portion of the sperm she now carries within her will find their way into a small pocket within her abdomen called a spermatheca, there to remain until released by the queen herself, a very little at a time over the course of her life, at the moment when an egg is passing by a valve in the pocket during its journey from her ovary through her oviducts and out her ovipositor. An egg thus fertilized will develop into an infertile female worker bee; eggs passing through the queen's oviducts without receiving a dollop of sperm will become drones.

So it happens, then, that although drones get to *be* fathers if they succeed in mating, they themselves have no fathers. (They do have a grandfather, on their queen mother's side.) On the other hand, all workers in a given colony—any one of which could have been made to grow into a queen, if fed the right diet in its infancy—do have fathers, though not usually all the same one. In genetic terms, the workers are diploid (blessed with a full complement of chromosomes, half from one parent and half from another) and the drones haploid (endowed with only one set of chromosomes); the whole arrangement is called haplodiploidy. This means that some of the workers are full sisters to one another (same pair of parents), some are half-sisters (same mother, different father), and all are half-sisters to the drones. The queen's apparent promiscuity—her deliberate mating with more than a handful of males—ensures a measure of genetic diversity within the hive, which in turn may help the colony to withstand any nasty surprises nature decides to throw its way: if disease, for instance, were to be visited upon the whole family at once, some of them might have the genetic wherewithal to escape unscathed.

This condition of haplodiploidy also holds some significance for the honeybees' famously social nature. Because there are so very many more sisters in the hive than half-sister-and-brother combos, "kinship selection" readily kicks in: the more closely related bees are genetically programmed to be more protective of and cooperative with one another than with bees to which they are less related. Makes a lot of sense, when you figure it's the females doing all the work of the colony, and lots of it, yet without bickering among themselves or getting seriously in one another's way. It may also help to explain why the girls can evict the boys from the hive in the fall with no discernible reluctance or regret whatsoever: were they fully related as sisters and brothers, this fratricidal purging of the hive might not be so readily accomplished (once evicted, a drone necessarily starves to death). And why this apparently cruel turn among the workers? Simple economics. Since no queens in the general vicinity will be launching nuptial flights over the winter, no drones will be necessary till next spring, yet keeping them around in the meanwhile would be costly in terms of honey stores, which the colony needs to get it through the lean months. Much more pragmatic to be rid of these couch potatoes now and wait till February or thereabouts to encourage the queen to lay a few hundred new drone eggs.

I know, I know. Moments ago I said that the queen chooses the sex of her babes—nothing about workers "encouraging" her choice in one direction or another. And it's true, the queen does have final say, exercised via that business of sperm released selectively from her spermatheca. But the workers do what they can to influence royal policy in this matter: they build brood comb suggestive of one sex or the other. That is, when the queen comes upon an empty wax cell sized to house a worker, she lays a fertilized egg in it; when she comes upon a slightly larger cell, one made to the specifications of the comparatively larger drone, she usually takes the hint—time to think blue for a change rather than pink. *Ping,* she pops into it an unfertilized egg. What's more, if ever the workers are unhappy with the queen's choice in a given instance, they may express their feeling by promptly eating the larva in question: sex determination in the colony by abortion, you might say.

Because a beekeeper wants far more workers in the hive than drones, prefab wax foundation comes embossed only with the rudimentary makings of worker cells—so, in a way, the beekeeper, too, casts a vote in the queen's sex selection as she lays. Still, she'll occasionally lay a male egg, even if she has to do it in a worker cell; the drone larva's oversized body will therefore have to protrude from the face of the comb a little, like an overgrown teenager's feet hanging off the edge of a bed, giving this fellow a bulletlike shape when he gets sealed over with wax for pupation.

The influence a beekeeper tries to exercise over the queen's sex selection by providing foundation free of drone cells is a minor form of human meddling with the natural order of the hive, as is the whole business of setting the colony up in a clean, dry hive box with frames and foundation to begin with. When we so wish, we're capable of meddling far more intrusively. Consider artificial insemination: as with all intensively managed livestock, it occurs in the bee business somewhat routinely. The Lilliputian scale of the tools involved (a technician inserts an anesthetized queen headfirst into a clear tube, opens her vaginal orifice with instruments on either side called micromanipulators, and with a fine, glass pipette or a plastic syringe injects her with drone semen) has the paradoxical effect, for me, of magnifying the blunt fact that human desire is being imposed on wildness, with the unabashed goal of marking the genetic cards, as it were. As usual in such cases, the enterprise is suffused with good intentions. Say I run a large commercial apiary and can't afford to lose a portion of my hives every winter to that dastardly Varroa mite. Chances are I'll want to cash in on the work of researchers who have raised numerous virgin queens and replaced their Dionysian nuptial flights with arranged, monogamous marriages: that is, each queen has been artificially inseminated by a single drone apiece, one taken from a colony exhibiting suppressed mite reproduction, or SMR. Such colonies have been found to resist Varroa infestations through the influence of just two genes (or so the research currently suggests); whenever Varroa shows up among these bees, it doesn't reproduce well, so the honeybee mortality ordinarily associated with the mite is substantially reduced. Were I a businesswoman, I might understandably jump at the chance to re-queen all my hives with these new and improved, SMR-inseminated gals. And it might not occur to me to worry in the least that these queens' forced monogamy could itself be setting my hives up for new troubles: as each hive gradually becomes genetically uniform—with all the workers in a given colony sharing the same pair of parents—the bees therein might be trading increased resistance to Varroa for reduced resistance to something else.

Ah, well, suppose it does—call it job security for the entomologists, I guess, who will turn assiduously to new solutions as new difficulties arise. Still, it is worth remarking that the same basic condition, that of reduced genetic variability, obtains in all domesticated species, animal or plant, from house cats to horses and from cauliflower to cotton and everything in between. That's why they generally need human care—protection from the elements and disease in many animal cases, protection from weeds and insect pests in most plant cases, artificial feeding programs in both— because the traits that once helped them manage as wild creatures have been bred out of them. Often by accident, while we were trying to beef up (as it were) some other traits that we happened to like. Sweetness in carrots, for example, or fast weight gain in chickens.

Such tinkering—artificial selection—when used by British pigeon breeders of the nineteenth century to achieve prize-winning results, was one of the inspirations for Darwin's great insight into how evolution works. We've been doing it, with varying degrees of intentionality, for eons, at least since the first farmers guessed at the improvements to be gained by saving seed from the biggest and tastiest of their food crops. To such efforts do we owe potatoes the size of a fist rather than a pea, and cucumbers free of bitterness; to them do we owe the very creation of many of our most familiar food sources, including corn (the product of crossed grasses) and cattle (descended from a type of water buffalo).

Although "domesticated" in a similar sense, specially bred honeybees differ from most other livestock in one crucial respect, described earlier in these pages: they are allowed to roam the world at large, and sometimes they

exploit the privilege by not coming back. Thus it is probably no stretch to suggest that an artificially mated queen
and her progeny, once the urge to go feral grabs them (and
supposing it remains unchecked by a beekeeper), will now
and then take the handiwork of humanity with them and
pass it around in nature, in whatever corner of the world
they happen to find themselves. Case in point: that "killer"
bee, the Africanized honeybee, with which Brazilian researchers were fiddling some fifty years ago in order to produce a line of livestock adapted to the South American
climate. There would appear to be no end to the things that
will seep, on occasion, out of Pandora's jar.

Selective breeding is just one of many hundreds, if not
thousands, of ways human beings have changed the world
they came to dominate so many centuries ago. The fancy
term is anthropogenic (human-induced) change. Though
much of it seems positive, the rest can leave a body feeling
a little sick, as one would in the face of a terrible desecra-
tion of some kind.

Quite a number of the changes we've wrought happened by accident: plant seeds or egg cases crossed whole
oceans in someone's trouser cuffs, and the next thing anybody knew, an invasive weed or insect was running the locals off their own turf. A good bit happened on purpose,
usually when we were trying to improve our own lot in
some way—to patch up some of those cracks in nature that
Emerson spoke of—so as to obtain more food, protection,
or comfort. Early natives across parts of eastern North
America set fire to the woods periodically to clear out the
underbrush and flush out game animals, which practice

eventually yielded fire-adapted ecosystems that hadn't been there before; early modern Europeans paid dearly for ton upon ton of imported beaver fur to warm their beds, coaches, and wagons in winter, inadvertently changing dramatically the amount and location of countless North American wetlands, simply because beaver-dam building had slowed nearly to a halt. And of course, the Industrial Revolution's many new technologies yielded, and continue to yield, great improvements in human health, long-distance communications, and travel, at the same time that they have remade our land into a place Pocahontas and her ilk would not recognize. To take just one related pair of examples: John Deere invented a mechanical means of achieving traction in a farm field, and not long afterward some kindred spirit of his invented deep-drilling irrigation. Since machines—unlike horses or oxen—don't need to take time out for meals or sleep, it wasn't long before virtually all of the Great Plains prairie ecosystems had been converted to something resembling, from an airplane, an elaborate game board. Further examples could be cited ad infinitum. With each passing year, it seems the sunsets are a little more lurid (thanks to layers of air pollution) and the permafrost near the planet's poles a little softer (climate change, thought by most scientists to be at least partly anthropogenic in origin). Even the look of outer space is changing, as more and more detritus from our space programs—discarded satellites, rockets, and assorted paraphernalia—floats through the cold black ether.

Still, we mean well in so many of these and countless other instances of human fiddling; and of course, since we are animals in our own right, it must be expected that we'll change our surroundings to some degree, as most animals do. Although I'd often like to shake a righteous fist and scream at the infidels to leave off mucking around with God's grand universe, I can't do it without risking a touch of hypocrisy. Setting aside for the moment the crucial fact that greed more than need drives a great many of our changes—the captains of industry are locked by economic logic into an endless cycle of rapacity, with no room simply to say "Okay, enough"—I'm as implicated as anyone in many of the changes continually under way. I appreciate the way my car has made the mountains low and the valleys smooth; I like having reasonably clean water available at the touch of a tap. I, too, sport a pair of opposable thumbs and a capacity for seeing not just what is, but also what could be. I'm thankful for what others have accomplished in the way of patching up the cracks in our otherwise wonderful home, and I want to pitch in and do my own share of the work—the little improvements I might bring to this big old lovely third rock from the sun, with which I seem always to be carrying on a lovers' quarrel.

Some Christians speak of the original Fall as "fortunate," for it gave us, as the Milton scholar Stanley Fish says, "something to do." Fields to cultivate, cattle to invent, distances to bridge, brokenness to heal. Meaningful work, and the chance to find meaning in one's work. In short, as some would have it, a whole world to help Divine Mind to fully realize.

III.

Along about my second or third year of keeping bees in Maine, I set up a small observation hive under the protection of our screened back porch, fitted with a clear plastic tube protruding from the hive and out to the larger world—a means of egress and ingress for the bees—through an opening I created in one window screen. Keeping bees without also keeping an observation hive is done by some, I suppose, though for the life of me I can't imagine why: like choosing an aisle rather than a window seat on an airplane flight, it seems like such a missed opportunity. An observation hive has two glassed sides fitted into a wooden stand sized to hold one (sometimes two, in an upper story) frame of wax foundation and a couple hundred honeybees. To get such a miniature colony going, you take a frame of comb from a regular, functioning hive to insert between the glass walls—but not just any frame. You want one with a goodly amount of capped brood on it, so you can be sure of new, young bees emerging over the first few weeks to help keep the mini-hive going, and, most important, you want it to contain as well a dozen or more freshly laid eggs, so the bees can raise a queen. Assuming, of course, that you are not taking the larger hive's queen from her home, which would be, frankly, a lousy idea. The new colony will need its own queen, certainly, and with fresh eggs on hand, it will soon have one; the beauty of glass is, you can watch her, and all the other newborns to come, being raised.

Aware within hours of their queenless situation, the honeybees in the little hive will choose a female egg that's just a couple of days old and begin feeding it generous quantities of royal jelly. Royal jelly is a glandular secretion of the nurse bees similar to what they feed all developing grubs but higher in substances such as pantothenic acid and biopterin, chemicals that will make the royal difference as the egg develops. And this queen-to-be will get lots more of the stuff than would a developing worker or drone. She also gets a larger apartment all to herself: whereas worker and drone eggs spend their infancy in wax cells equal in size to or only slightly larger than cells used for storing nectar and pollen, a growing queen gets a sort of full-body sling, a dimpled wax cell hanging to one side of and an inch or so down the face of the comb, suggestive of an unshelled peanut.

Social caste and sex entirely aside, all developing brood hatches from the egg stage on about Day 3 as larvae, with no other purpose or desire than to eat. A honeybee grub is basically just a set of intestines encased in a pearly white jacket, with a mouth at one end and an anus at the other. For about five or six days it puts on weight and, periodically, molts its outer shell, to give it more room for growing; then the nurse bees leave off their feeding and cap the cell, giving the little one within some dark, quiet privacy—which even my glass walls couldn't penetrate—in which to spin a cocoon and pupate. Over the next several days the same miracle occurs that for centuries has inspired wonder, poetry, and religious awe, as the plain, fat little worm we last observed becomes a black and gold bit of intricate, shivering life, complete with circulatory, nervous, respiratory, digestive, reproductive (in all but the workers), and endocrine systems, not to mention eyes, antennae, legs, thorax, stinger (in the females), body hair, and dainty, transparent wings.

You can just about set your watch by each bee's emergence as an adult: a queen takes, typically, sixteen days to go from egg to grown-up, a worker bee twenty-one days, and a drone twenty-four. (These numbers describe the Italians, anyway; the Africanized bees emerge a day or two sooner, yet another reason AHB stays ahead of the competition.) And with an observation hive, it's possible to witness the exciting moment as the wax cap is slowly ripped apart from inside. Antennae soon poke through, then those big eyes, then the whole head and the front legs, churning mightily at the air and the edges of the cell for traction. *Et voilà,* there he or she is, reporting for duty. Technically, the newborn still isn't a mature adult; there's one more molt to undergo within a few days, and until that happens, the inner organs are rushing to become fully themselves, especially in the reproductive systems of the queen and the drones.

For the rest of their lives, these latter two types of bees will not change much. The workers, on the other hand, are endowed with a more fluid, protean physiology, which enables them to morph their way through the long series of roles necessary to keep the entire organism—the colony itself—thriving.

Without question, that little glass hive of mine on the back porch was one of the highlights of my years in the

Maine farmhouse. Besides watching new bees emerge while I perched in a rickety wooden chair pulled up to the table on which the hive sat, I lost happy, self-forgetting hours to spying on workers coming and going through the plastic tube; beneath it, I'd rigged up a kind of landing strip with duct tape and stiff cardboard, which dipped a little with the weight of each arriving bee. Some came home laden with pellets of orange or buttery yellow pollen in their little back-leg baskets. Others weren't visibly laden with anything, but their behavior with the house bees gave them away: approached by another worker and tapped on the head by inquiring antennae, such a returning forager would open her mandibles and, presumably (this was very hard to see clearly), regurgitate into the receiving mouth of a house bee whatever sweet trace of the larger world's life she'd managed to procure in the preceding hours. The recipient would then head for the larder—the open rows of nectar-bearing cells at the top of the comb—to unload her loot. Meanwhile, other bees were building or repairing wax comb, cleaning out empty cells, or carrying the dead bees that had dropped to the bottom toward the plastic tube for removal, work that was no doubt harder in this circumstance than it would have been in an ordinary hive; the tube being some eight inches long and not very spacious, it was more challenging to negotiate than the simple wooden lip that my bees out in the back field had for a front door. And of course, given the glass walls and just one frame of bees within, I was pretty sure to find the queen any time I wanted to, a luxury not nearly so available with an ordinary hive. Had I known at the time to keep up a really careful watch in the first few days after the new queen's emergence, I might have seen her depart on her nuptial flight. But it passed me by.

Even if you've never been to Maine you've probably heard or guessed that the winters can get, ah, cold. As in, brutally, inhumanly, insanely cold. Pipe-bursting, fingers-sticking-to-the-garage-door cold. A honeybee hive with just one frame stands not a chance of getting through that season if left out on a screened porch, where even people wearing long johns and parkas and wool caps do not linger more than a few minutes, for six months of the year. Unlike a more typical colony, an observation hive has no massive population of bees with which to form a winter cluster for warmth, nor the necessary room for such a maneuver. So as the summer waned, I had to consider what next. Should I just let this little living community die a natural death out on the porch, on one of the first freezing September nights? Not an appealing proposition. Should I try putting the frame back into the outdoor hive, sans queen, since each colony will usually tolerate only one? Also not an option: when I'd removed this frame of bees, I'd replaced it with a new one with fresh foundation, which was sure to be full of bees now. And besides, the girls in the big house would not readily accept bees they no longer recognized as be-longing among them, so, even if there had been room to do it, adding now unfamiliar bees to a self-sufficient, self-contained hive would likely result in a nasty little war.

A third possibility also had its drawbacks, but they seemed surmountable. I could bring the observation hive into the house and keep it alive through most of the winter.

The tricky considerations were mainly two. First, whether my husband would consent to having the thing inside at all, fastened by means of steel C-clips to the edge of my old oak desk in my study upstairs, right near a window that would have to be retooled, in a sense. And second, whether I could in fact retool said window in such a way as to let the bees leave when necessary (even in winter, they'll fly now and then to void their bowels) but not let in too much of the winter cold.

The first issue proved relatively simple to get past, as Mark could be pretty easygoing about my schemes so long as they didn't have to involve him. (He hadn't forgotten that night in Carolina when we'd paid a price for trying to move a colony that didn't appreciate the attention; when I needed his help again a couple of years later to move another hive, this one at the Maine place, he agreed only reluctantly, dressing first in his heavy winter parka; two thickly padded, mismatched snowmobiler's gloves; and a big black snowmobiler's helmet with tinted visor that we'd somehow acquired without also acquiring a snowmobile. This was in early August, so we had to move fast just to keep him from keeling over with heatstroke.) The second problem was a little matter of engineering: I raised the window about four inches, and fitted into the gap a thick piece of insulating Styrofoam, securing the edges all around with duct tape (which needed frequent refreshing over the next several months). With a pocketknife I cut a hole in the ridged foam the size of a quarter, and worked the plastic tube stretching from the hive into this. I didn't push it all the way through, figuring that the last half inch of the Styrofoam hole could serve as a tiny, curved landing pad for any arriving bee. Though the bees would probably manage without one if they had to, it seemed to me a courtesy always to provide a little something of this sort if possible.

Human life during a Maine winter plays out chiefly indoors. Most of mine during that particular winter was spent upstairs in that study, chin in hands and gaze transfixed. As the weeks went by, marked by chilly rains, increasingly heavy frosts, then periodic snowfalls, and eventually, a brief January thaw that left a hard, crusty rind on the snowpack, the bees in my study bumped and buzzed their little lives away. By late February the whole lot were pretty much history, queen included (she had it in her to live longer, but needed attendant bees to feed her). And so I lost another hive, not surprisingly, but at least not—for a change!—through any overtly stupid moves on my part. Friends to whom I mentioned this measured, steady attrition teased me for being a honeybee killer, unable or unwilling to believe me when I pointed out that those particular bees wouldn't have fared any better in the bigger hive. No summer- or early fall–born bee makes it to the following spring; a colony is perennial thanks only to the eggs laid in very late fall. These emerge in winter darkness and hang on, waiting for better days. But since my little housebroken hive didn't have much of a workforce in the nursery, the youngsters starved in their beds for want of attention. In a sense, then, maybe I was a honeybee killer, after all, though certainly more through thoughtlessness than malice.

Who can say what a beginning is, much less when? Everything begins in medias res. The story of spring in northern

New England always seems less like a beginning than a slow, tortuous ending, and it sounds like dripping water. Ice releasing its grip on the eaves; granular, debris-sprinkled snow retreating in an even, steamy circle from the trunks of trees; puddles speckling over with the teensy black bodies of snow fleas, and leaking at the edges. Patches of pale, soggy grass reappear. Pussy willows stand at attention in the vicinity of bogs still frozen everywhere but the margins. Sugar maples sprout galvanized tin buckets for catching the sap that races upward on warming days, and back down to underground safety on chilly nights.

To hear the Roman poet Ovid tell it in *The Metamorphoses,* written early in the first century c.e., the whole business of seasonal shifts originated during the silver age of the world's ancient infancy: the era immediately following that first, perfect golden age. Reworking the themes Hesiod had treated, Ovid suggests the golden age was one long, soft spring, when gentle winds prevailed and when fields "grew white with ripening grain"; rivers flowed with milk, and honey dripped from the trees. The bronze and iron ages succeeded the silver, introducing into the world increasing violence among men, a period when "purity, truth, and trust all fled," when crime and betrayal, and greed and warfare, became the orders of the day. "A man hoped for his wife's early death, and she hoped for her husband's," Ovid writes; "a son too soon asked his father how old he was." In disgust, Zeus sent a mighty flood over the earth to rid it of these god-awful mortals. Once again, as they had been in the earliest dawn of creation, "land and sea were one." The deluge spared just one good man and one woman, so it became their special burden to repopulate the earth with their kind—not by conceiving children, but by casting stones over their shoulders, each of which softened before their eyes and took the shape of a person. Other living beings sprang from the mud left behind by the receding floodwaters. Thus did the planet resume once again the work of becoming itself.

And so on, world without end—for as long as our guiding star holds out, anyway—populated from hill and dale and across the eons by all manner of beings that would be better named with verbs than with nouns. Because, like it or not, as others have often noted and as Darwin in particular made plain, what we're all born into is an order in which change and changeability are the only constants. Generation upon generation of lives and loves won but soon lost, or rather, borrowed and too soon returned, lives of all improbable kinds cobbled together from the merest earth and water into flesh and bone, feather and fin, scale and shell, thorax and wing, leaf and petal. Earth and water, earth and sweet, sweet water. Like your own familiar front door, like your easiest easy chair, these always seem perfectly ready and beautifully fashioned to do the honors, to welcome every last one of us back into the grand, ineffable scheme of things.

6

Nesting

Last night when I was asleep
I dreamt, blessed illusion!,
that I had a beehive
within my heart;
and in it the golden bees
were elaborating
with old and bitter things,
white wax and honey sweet.

—ANTONIO MACHADO, POEM LIX,
Solitudes, Galleries, and Other Poems
(translated from the Spanish by Richard L. Predmore)

This part caught me by surprise: the hot, inescapable glare of too much late-summer sun. Various other signs that something extraordinary had passed through this way came as no surprise at all; born near New Orleans and raised on the Gulf Coast, I'd seen their like before. Jackson was about where they began to show up: the downed limbs and occasional split tree trunk, the peeled billboards at the side of the highway, the power lines swinging low in great loops from leaning poles. The farther I drove, the more frequent and terrible the signs: metal roofs ripped from the tops of stores and warehouses; church spires bent or torn altogether away; swaths of pine trees snapped in half at about the same twenty-foot height, their crowns all falling northward; windows of cars, homes, and storefronts alike smashed; boats, trailers, and riding lawnmowers carried off to odd destinations—a motel swimming pool or the exposed bottom of an overturned delivery van. Past Hattiesburg, I had to keep a close lookout for whatever debris still lay across the highway. And I had to stay on the alert for any gas stations open for business. Mostly, you saw from a quarter mile away the pump handles hooded with plastic shopping bags to signify they were out of order. Now and then the bags bobbed in a puff of air, too hot to warrant the name breeze.

Drawing closer to the Escatawpa River, I worried the bridge might be out. Although others had been reported wrecked or washed away, this one, to my knowledge, had made neither the national news nor the state department of transportation website I'd been checking for word on road conditions; no news, I hoped, was good news in this instance. Sure enough, the bridge proved intact, if incongruously decorated here and there by an open, soiled suitcase and a child's soggy teddy bear, among less recognizable trash. Driving up toward the crest—bridges around here tend to be steeply arched, to accommodate shipping traffic—I strained for a glimpse of the industrial docks at the marshy edges of the river below, but the guardrails got in the way. I pressed on. Increasingly dense development lining the highway soon meant increasing degrees of havoc: the tattered remnants of fast-food outlets, chain hotels, and gas stations. Now lines of cars could be seen creeping through large parking lots, a couple of them belonging to churches, where volunteers were handing out ice, diapers, canned goods, and bottled water by the case. By the time I passed under Interstate 10 and pulled closer to its older, east–west counterpart, State Highway 90, I was caught up in a slow-moving caravan of vehicles myself: these local roads, just two miles north of the beach where Hurricane Katrina came ashore, had only recently been reopened to traffic by the authorities, and now the storm surge had been replaced by a human one.

These last couple of miles into Pascagoula thus became the slowest of my five-hundred-mile trip. To conserve gasoline I switched off the air conditioner and rolled down the car windows. That sun, that relentless sun—there was no dodging it, for at this hour (around five in the afternoon) it was low enough in the sky to burn through all my windows. At first all this light seemed puzzling, unfamiliar . . . and then I got it. For decades to come, there will be in thousands of coastal residents' minds a Before Katrina and an After Katrina, and one difference to be remarked will surely be the way broad, dappled blankets of Southern shade were swept away all at once when the moiling, wind-churned floodwaters took with them the area's generous share of pines, pin oaks, and magnolias, among other species. Even the coast's thousands of live-oak trees—ordinarily a match for just about anything, as their fat ancient trunks and wide, gracefully draping crowns typically attest—gave up the ghost in vast numbers this time. And what trees still stood might not for long: everywhere you turned, the vegetation was as crispy brown as if torched, though in truth it had drowned. Mere river water alone would likely have been less devastating, but river water had mingled with city sewage and the salty waters vomited up by the Mississippi Sound. Which also partially explained the stench; the rest of *that* story lay in the rotting remains of flooded refrigerators, thousands of pounds of lost animal and vegetable life that would never nourish a single human one.

I didn't head straight for my mother's place. Cell phone calls, when they'd gotten through, had assured me she was okay and that her house, though seriously damaged, still stood. Once there, I'd be throwing myself into the work of cleaning up, but I wanted first to get the lay of the land at ground zero, as it were. So I drove the beachfront boulevard—at least, the section of it that hadn't washed away—lying just a block beyond my mother's residence, and at the five-mile-per-hour creep necessitated by all the construction debris, fallen trees, and chunks of the city's public fishing pier that spilled into or lay across the road. Several of the houses along this boulevard had been genuinely antebellum, the loveliest of them (to me) in the Creole-cottage style found nowhere else but southern Mississippi and Louisiana. Some had been much more contemporary, split-leveled and faced with quite a lot of glass to admit sweeping ocean views. Now all were either blasted to rubble or utterly washed away. With one amazing exception: the oldest of them, a stately Greek Revival set back from the road and flanked by a generous spread of formerly shaded and carefully tended grounds, still stood firm, though it bore obvious damage—broken windows and wooden shutters, among other wounds. This was the Longfellow House, an inn named for the poet who had once spent time here, and a locally popular spot for staging family photographic sessions (including one my mother had put my brother and me through some thirty years before), weddings, retirement parties, and the like.

To pass the Longfellow House was to enter far more desolate territory. When I looked to my right, it was to see people picking through their shattered lives: a girl's mangled bicycle; a splintered grandfather clock; a water-swollen dictionary; a file cabinet smashed beyond opening; a soaked mattress; a mud-caked, overstuffed, and thoroughly waterlogged easy chair; the battered remnant of a clothes dryer, its belly still full of the shirts and blouses, now soiled beyond recovery, that the family had left unattended in their haste to evacuate. The tank tops, shorts, and running shoes these newly homeless wore, muddied by all that poking among their sorry heaps of belongings, were now the only clothing they'd have until relatives or relief workers could bring them other people's castoffs.

I looked left: things appeared just as they'd always been. A thin strip of blond sand, inexplicably free of debris. A broad stretch of dark water, scalloped and gently silvered by wavelets, and scouted from overhead by small squadrons of pelicans, their heads pulled back into their shoulders, necks thrust forward into a pronounced S. The shimmering profiles of distant barrier islands, marking the southernmost edge of the sound.

Back again to the right: whole roofs lay atop foundation slabs, the houses that should have come between having simply vanished. Grass that should have been bright green wore instead a uniformly dark gray wash of mud, and driveways crackled underfoot with the stuff: a two- or three-inch layer of it had lain in the sun for a week and baked dry. A matching pair of brick staircases swept in elegant curves upward to meet each other at . . . nothing, or almost nothing. Searching in particular for the homes of high school friends, I came up empty in nearly every instance, or thought I did—it was hard to be sure of my bearings, with so many familiar landmarks now gone or buried under great piles of uprooted trees, shredded drywall, blasted brick and mortar, bed-size shards of glass, and lumpy strips of wet pink insulation suggestive of flayed flesh. I kept expecting to recognize someone among the rubble rakers, but no. A thirtysomething woman's hair spilled out of a slipshod ponytail. A paunchy man stopped pulling hard at a large, ruined rug caught under the mess that was once his house, evidently to mop his face with a bandana. Everywhere the sun beat fiercely down with real physical pressure, or glanced painfully off the bright metal sides of things no longer identifiable. It seemed vaguely obscene—all that sunlight, bleaching bare, suddenly exposed wooden studs as it might the broken, vulture-picked bones strewn about a desert wasteland.

The drivable asphalt soon giving out, I executed a careful three-point turn to head out of there the way I'd come. For a brief moment, my windshield filled with the wide, sparkling Gulf, another cruising pelican, and out at the edge of the world, the miragelike barrier islands.

With so much human misery crying out for attention

from New Orleans clear over to Mobile, what room has the heart left over for the millions of animals that must surely also have lost life, limb, or at the very least, home? We often forget that birds, squirrels, rabbits, opossums, frogs, fish, even colonies of bees—feral or kept—must also flee before the onslaught of a great storm, and that many cannot run or fly or swim fast enough. In the days following the disaster, you occasionally heard of alligators and water moccasins showing up many miles away from their usual haunts, often to the shock and dismay of some home-owner already shaken out of his wits. As children in Sunday school, we're told that the bird has its nest and the fox its den, but that the Son of Man had nowhere to lay his head—a circumstance neatly foreshadowed by his birth in a borrowed manger. But with last December's South Asian tsunami, the arrival in the United States this year of Katrina and then Hurricane Rita soon after, followed by mudslides in Guatemala and a massive earthquake in Kashmir, then record-setting floods in the American Northeast—well, I can't help thinking that in many parts of the world, even the bird and the fox are pretty hard up. Homelessness now appears the default condition of all concerned.

Beekeepers have traditionally gone to some trouble to ensure their bees have decent homes; indeed, to keep bees hanging around at all presupposes just such an effort. But setting the bees up in digs to their liking is really only half the challenge. The other half is making sure you can occasionally plunder their pantry without wrecking it and chasing off or otherwise harming the colony.

Honeybee aficionados are fond of calling L. L. Langstroth, a nineteenth-century minister from Ohio, the patron saint of modern beekeeping, on account of the remarkable hive he patented in 1852, the basic design of which prevails across the Western world to this day. In fairness, one might note that Langstroth stood on the shoulders of dozens of tinkerers who had gone before him, several of them men of the cloth like himself. (One of them, Christopher Wren, became, later in life, Britain's great seventeenth-century architect.) The problem all these beekeepers or friends of the beekeeper set out to solve was this: How do you rob a colony of its honey without simultaneously destroying the wax comb in which the honey is always stored, and perhaps lots of bees in the process? For centuries, beekeepers had done just that; really, they'd had no choice. But from the point of view of anyone who wanted to harvest honey from a given colony not just once but again a few weeks later, and yet again the following season, this approach was like burning down the barn and maiming or killing the cow to get a pail of milk. For early beekeepers, a new colony of bees complete with wax nest might have been easier to come by than a new cow and barn, but it was nevertheless an expensive undertaking in time and energy, that of both keeper and bee. (Make no mistake: a hive's many pounds of wax represent a tremendous investment of honeybee energy, which is also to say, many months of collective honeybee life span.) And besides, people would usually prefer not to wait for extended periods between their sugar fixes—that is, between jars of honey.

To appreciate the design that Langstroth perfected,

which effectively solved the riddle, consider first what sort of nest honeybees create in nature, when left to their own devices. (Among species and varieties, nesting habits and nest structure can differ somewhat; the following pertains chiefly to *Apis mellifera*.) It is made entirely of wax that the bees themselves have extruded out of their own bodies, one thin, teensy flake at a time—no twigs, leaves, or bits of string to be gathered, as for so many other animals' nests, including those of many insects. The warm wax flakes are pressed together, molded into row upon row of nearly uniform hexagonal cells, each about a half inch deep; this is called drawing out comb. The cells will soon cradle nectar, water, pollen, finished honey, eggs, and larvae. Together, hundreds of adjacent cells in turn compose a comb, with the back wall of any given cell serving, on its other side, as the back wall to another cell facing in the opposite direction. And how's this for smart planning: these back-to-back cells are always made to angle slightly upward and away from one another, presumably to prevent anything stored within from spilling out the end, so long as the cells remain uncapped. Several combs together—fashioned parallel to one another, with about three eighths of an inch of open space between them ("bee space") and all attached along their tops to a thick, connecting bridge of solid wax—make up a nest. Almost inevitably, it will be found in a cavity of some sort, such as a hollow tree, or maybe some deep recess in the side of a cliff. Still more wax and plenty of propolis do the job of securing the nest to the inner walls, and sometimes to the upper ceiling as well, if there is one, of the cavity.

Because the combs always came attached to one another and to the cavity, getting at their contents without cutting them apart was for centuries virtually impossible, whether the container in question was in fact a hollow tree, a crevice in a rock, or one of dozens of artificial hives that beekeepers used through the ages, such as the picturesque, upside-down straw basket known as a skep, especially popular across the English countryside.

Enter at stage left the many practical minds of the nineteenth century, and Langstroth's modular, removable-frame hive. Langstroth recognized that a satisfactory design would freely allow the bees to build their combs downward, as they do in nature, but not from a connecting bridge of wax at the top: rather, the beekeeper would provide several slender bars of lightweight wood, laid parallel to one another and across the open top of a square box, also made of wood. Further, each of these top bars would become the top edge of a rectangular wooden frame, with the bars all along the sides and bottom giving the bees a sturdy structure to which they could attach their comb, discouraging them from attaching it to the walls of the hive. These frames of comb all hang together from two recessed ledges built into the box and lying just below the hive's removable inner cover, very much as office files do in a hanging-file cabinet. (An additional, outer cover later goes on over the top of the box.) And this, too, Langstroth stressed: honeybee nest specifications require that these frames hang three eighths of an inch apart from one another as well as from the hive walls and the cover, so as to preserve that all-important bee space—empty corridors, essentially, that the

bees insist upon and naturally provide for themselves during nest construction in nature, to ensure ease of movement through the hive.

Now the beekeeper can easily pull one comb (one
frame) out at a time—to inspect it, or to rob it of sweet
treasure—and just as readily put it back for reuse by the
bees. No fuss, no muss. Most important, no need for the
bees to spend precious time and energy building new
comb; that energy, itself fueled by the nectar they've gathered and eaten, can now be channeled into activity highly
desirable to a beekeeper, the gathering of yet more nectar
to make yet more honey.

Not only did Langstroth make beekeeping easier than
ever before with his innovative hive, then, he also made it
very productive, and those increased surpluses in turn
spawned the birth of a very sweet commerce indeed.

Still another crucial aspect of nest construction had to
be allowed for, however, before Langstroth could say he
had a near perfect hive design. As noted, bees use their
hexagonal cells for storing several kinds of goods, but
they're organized about it: like a homeowner setting up
kitchen cupboards, bees choose to store brood over here in
this part of the hive, honey in this other part, pollen over
there, and so on. More precisely, a pulled frame of comb
from a one-story (one "deep super") hive will exhibit con-
centric, arched bands of cells containing—in this order,
from the top down—finished honey, unfinished (unripe)
honey, pollen, and brood, with the occasional cell here and
there holding simply water. The lion's share of the comb
(its bottom two thirds, say) is reserved for rearing brood.
Now, give the bees a second or third story—stacked supers

added to the original one—and they will feel they can spread their belongings out a bit, expanding both their own numbers and the quantity of goods needed to support the growing colony. Yet they will stick to their usual organizational pattern: brood down below, ripe honey way up top.

Thus Langstroth's modular design enables a beekeeper to take away the top box of a multiple-storied hive periodically, and in so doing to take away only honey-filled combs, without disturbing the all-important brood nest down cellar. But she must first force thousands of bees out of the top story and downstairs (so to speak), by one of a handful of means. My method is to place a thin, flat, specially designed board of the same length and width as the supers between the top super and the one just below it, and then to leave it there for a few days. The board has in its center an elaborate "bee escape" screen, which allows bees in the top super to pass into the lower super, but which does not allow passage in the opposite direction. In a few days' time the top super will be nearly bee free, so that when I take it and its sweet freight away from the hive, I don't risk getting mauled by any more than, say, a dozen or so stray bees (there's no getting them *all* out of your way). The whole super, lingering (doomed) bees and all, goes straight into a deep freezer in my garage for safekeeping, until I can make time to run the frames through my extractor. This is the other key item that makes beekeeping and honey production what they are today: basically it's a centrifuge, a metal drum with a wire cage inside that can hold vertical frames of honeycomb—which have first had their wax cappings sliced off with a warm, broad-bladed knife—safely suspended within the drum while I crank away at a handle attached to the cage's top. Centrifugal force spins the honey out to the sides of the drum, whence it slides down toward a valve at the bottom (the "honey gate") and out into a clean bottling tank (another metal drum, this one equipped not with a wire cage but with a cheesecloth filter), from there finally to slip and ooze into clear mason jars.

Now the combs have only a little residual honey left within them, which the bees will happily lap up when the frames go back into their super and atop the hive. Again, the significant fact here to note, from a beekeeper's perspective: the combs are intact, and immediately ready for reuse.

When I rounded the corner to enter my mother's street, relief mingled with amazement as I noted that nearly all the houses here still stood—this just a tenth of a mile north of those bombed-out beachfront homes. Had the storm been instantly robbed of some of its power by the resistance those first buildings had tried to offer? I wondered. Certainly, the houses I now passed—two-story brick affairs, for the most part—had been badly damaged by the high winds and the storm surge that had washed over the land, the southernmost ones to the point of total loss. Those clad in pale bricks, such as my mother's cream-colored one, bore a waist-high water mark all around. But the majority of these houses were still on their foundations, and still had most of their walls and roofs. The debris lining this street, then, chiefly comprised the ruined remains of things that

had been hauled out of the flooded first floors and the
drenched, roofless second floors: sodden carpets, oriental
rugs, and sofas; ooze-covered stereos, TVs, videos and
DVDs as well as their players, computers, lamps, water
heaters, kitchen appliances of all sorts, kitchen cabinets,
coats and belts and shoes among other clothing, purses and
fancy hats, towels and bedding, photograph albums (the
photos within all bled of color and form), books and book-
shelves, children's toys, fine china and silver and the side-
boards that had held them. Plus every possible item you
can imagine ever finding in an American garage—sports
and camping equipment, shovels and rakes and bags of fertilizer, woodworking tools, bags of dog food. Sections of
privacy fencing, ripped from its posts. Large, decorative
clay garden pots, most of them cracked or smashed altogether. Newly potless ferns, cacti, and other assorted
plants. Teak patio tables and canvas umbrellas, now
busted at the legs and torn from their poles. Ragged shreds
of cloth and plastic trash, festooning the branches of dying
shrubs and trees.

Up and down the block there appeared numerous,
hastily made plywood signs propped up in front yards.
Some simply named the family, house number, and the in-
surance company they were hoping would visit soon:
THOMASON, 838, STATE FARM. Others attested to the law-
lessness these residents had feared in the first days after the
storm, when neither streetlights nor routine police patrols
could be counted on: YOU LOOT, I SHOOT. Ever a creative
and gifted decorator, my mother had made up her own
macabre version of the message. After removing the back

panel from a soaked and split wardrobe that now stood in her yard, she had turned it around and affixed to the opening a puppet of a wizened old woman, in whose arms Mom had artfully placed a wooden stick to suggest a shotgun aiming at all comers. ARMED AND PISSED, read the plywood sign posted a few feet away. (No empty threat, coming from our half-Italian matriarch, whom we call Mama Lupo; a former skeet shooter, she still keeps a rifle handy, and sees little reason to distinguish between a clay pigeon and a would-be thief.) Just across the street, the mood was lighter, though still black in its way: a muddied mattress leaning against a tree bore the spray-painted enticement YARD SALE—DIRT CHEAP.

My mother's driveway was the first to sport the formerly unthinkable, in this neighborhood ordinarily preoccupied with class pretensions: a recreational vehicle. Eventually several others would appear as well, as would mobile trailers provided by the Federal Emergency Management Agency, or FEMA, transforming the area into a modern American refugee camp, complete with folding chairs arranged under the RV awnings. (Periodic visits up and down the road by Red Cross vans calling out, via loudspeaker, the availability of hot meals or tetanus shots also contributed to the overall war-zone feel of things.) Besides giving residents a way to sleep protected overnight near their homes while they dedicated their days to cleaning up and rebuilding, the RVs came with their own generators: a negligible detail, perhaps, to anyone who's not from Dixie. But as long as gasoline could be had—relatives, like me, were carting in cans and cans of it from other states in our hatchbacks, aware it was nearly as precious a commodity to coastal residents as food and water—the RVs could supply electricity, which really came down to supplying just one indispensable necessity: air conditioning.

For all creatures great and small, nesting is primarily about securing comfortable shelter—from the elements, from predators, from noisy neighbors who would otherwise disturb one's rest. For most creatures, nesting is also about raising young in these protective conditions, and for some—honeybees and humans come to mind—it's about safely storing groceries as well, putting up a portion of the growing season's largesse against lean times to come. I'm often amazed to encounter young people, smart and old enough to be college students, stopped short by the surprising (to them) revelation that bees make honey for themselves, for their own nourishment, most importantly for their supply of winter calories. How can it not have occurred to them before that bees couldn't care less about our own, irrepressible attraction to this rich sweetener? Have these young adults also grown up believing a cow yields milk expressly to serve as an adjunct to peanut-butter sandwiches? Truth is, both cow and honeybee are making the only two foods found in nature made simply to *be* food, much of it (all of it, in the case of milk) especially intended for maturing young. Seeds, roots, stems, leaves, flowers, nuts, fruits, and animal flesh can also serve as food to countless creatures, but first they function as integral parts of the organisms from which they derive. The same cannot be said for either milk or honey.

Seen in this light, the phrase "milk and honey" may take on special resonance. But what, in fact, *is* honey? As already noted, it begins as nectar, the watery, sweet effusions of countless individual flowers, visited who knows how many times by how many bees. Nectar is composed primarily of sucrose and water, along with various minerals and vitamins present in trace amounts; present, too, could be traces of whatever humans might have applied to the flowers, for example a pesticide used in an apple orchard. To produce honey, the great majority of this nectar's water content will eventually have to be evaporated, during the ripening process within the hive. But first the nectar has to get to the hive, and it can get there by only one means, if it's to become honey: in the belly of a bee. Honey requires for its genesis a period of partial digestion, a brief window of time in which the nectar swishes about and mixes with honeybee saliva and stomach juices so the enzymes therein can perform an amazing act of alchemy. One of these enzymes is invertase, which inverts nearly all the nectar's sucrose into the simpler sugars fructose and glucose. (Another enzyme, glucose oxidase, makes its way into the honey but does nothing much unless or until that honey is later diluted with water, at which point it makes the antimicrobial hydrogen peroxide: hence honey's usefulness as a preservative in foods and as a salve for wounds.) Real honey cannot be humanly manufactured; only these insects can coax it forth, from the distilled essences of flowers—which in turn have seen their share of sun, soil, and rain, else there'd be no nectar to begin with—and from the tiny Crock-Pots of the bees' own bodies.

So while other Americans give their backyards over to

roses and cucumbers, or fill them with swimming pools and patio furniture and barbecue grills, I've surrendered mine to a handful of white wooden towers devoted to the manufacture of highly refined, richly matured—and fiercely desired, for nearly the whole of human history— bee spit.

Once, while gazing at my refrigerator, which was plastered with postcards and photographs I'd collected and snapped while traveling, my mother picked up on a pattern: a fondness for doors. I'd never noticed it before myself, but sure enough—there was the one taken in Megeve of an oak door with a sculpted iron hand affixed to the center for use as a knocker; another, also from France, depicted a leafy grapevine growing out of a cement pot on the ground against the house and twining luxuriously up over the doorway, its branches entangling the wrought iron of a second-floor balcony. Then there was the postcard featuring the triple, drab-green shuttered entrances of Lafitte's Blacksmith Shop, one of the oldest buildings in the New Orleans French Quarter, now serving as—what else?—a corner bar.

What's to be made of this doorway fetish, I sometimes wonder, if anything need be made of it? So far, nothing much.

But conscious now of this thing I seem to have for doors, it occurs to me that maybe that's why I fell for my current small abode on first sight: its front door. The dark, heavy wood alone probably wouldn't have held much appeal. But the top curves beautifully into an arch, and is graced up high by three little windows wedged together like slices of half a pie left in a pan, their rounded upper edges echoing the arch in the door. The doorway is flanked by irregular flagstones—dusky red, ocher, tan, and mustard—taken long ago from the nearby Arkansas River; the stones wrap protectively around the entire house, in fact. The combination of these stones and this door puts me in mind of a medieval castle gate, or of some mossy-roofed European cottage in deep woods, where one might expect to find Hansel and Gretel eyeing warily the witch intent upon enticing them inside.

In my neighborhood I'm the witch now, I suppose; just being single, female, middle-aged, intellectual, and rather introverted appears to be plenty of reason to qualify. Further incriminating would be all the plants and herbs in pots scattered about my wide porch and lining the steps, or sitting atop the stone balustrade beneath yet more arches. (Five wide arches in all, three in front and one each on the sides, together make for an arcade effect, and turn the porch into a cloister walk in miniature.) And of course there are the beehives in back, nearly as good as smoking cauldrons for keeping out the curious. Unless you're a cat: cats are fearless, and though I no longer own any myself (Ivy died, and Oscar went to live with friends in the country up north), an elderly woman nearby, another witch no doubt, feeds any stray that happens along, so of course ten or twenty of them have made every square foot of our short, narrow city block their own. Some are even midnight black: more witch effect, as if I needed that. Small wonder I have trouble attracting children to the door at Halloween, let alone eligible men the rest of the year. But down-and-outers? I seem to attract them just fine. One lives a few doors away but has taken to mounting my front porch steps occasionally—while I'm watering plants or otherwise puttering about—and turning to look out over the yard and street, breathing deeply and all but pounding his expanding chest in assumed ownership. I go along with his small talk but don't invite him in, wondering all the while to myself how it is that misfits like us don't exactly suit each other any more than we do the rest of the community all around.

The hard fact to be reckoned with in these, the Arkansas years (as I call them), is that making a home as a single person—more to the point, as a middle-aged divorcée—is a rather different undertaking from what making a home was as a young married woman. On the face of it, setting up house would appear easier now than before: no one's tastes or preferences but my own need be consulted as I decide which chair will rest where, which volumes will go into which of the living room's built-in, glass-fronted bookcases, or which rug will lie along which stretch of polished oak floor. And yet, and yet—now and then I still feel *him* looking over my shoulder, delivering himself of an opinion about where I've hung this watercolor, or set that reading lamp. (Now and then he comes to me in dreams, as if we've unfinished business between us, though chances are, only I think so.) Sometimes it seems I must have packed up the shambles of my life back in Maine a little too quickly, and in my haste failed to notice a ghost slither into one of the shipping cartons before it was sealed. Most of the time he keeps to himself down here in the Arkansas place, but as I say, not always.

Then there are those moments, which finally must

come, when I have to exit that heavy medieval door and encounter the street; this, too, I've come to believe is part of the work of nesting. And work it most certainly is. The simple fact of being a social animal makes for any human being a double-edged sword: on the one hand, we all have periods when we concur with Jean-Paul Sartre that hell is other people; some of us, no doubt, experience these more often than others. The trouble is, hell is also the *absence* of other people. Engagement with the world beyond our doorsteps does not come easily to everyone. Still, we must do it or die, by which I mean we must do a good deal more than make the occasional grocery store run.

Maybe part of me knew this when I chose, upon moving back South, to live not in the country this time but in the very heart of the village—you know, the one it takes to raise a child, or for that matter a grown and still growing woman. Without gregarious Mark handy to do the reaching out for both of us to rural neighbors, I could happily have holed up in the bottomland woods and gone slowly, ecstatically mad. Instead I reside now in the oldest part of this relatively quiet, unexceptional college town. On either side of my place and around the nearby corners, there are grandmotherly pensioners, blue-collar workers, small children, and young professionals, all of several races and nationalities, some of them émigrés from as far away as Pakistan and Indonesia. Any one of them is likely on any given day to delight or derange me. And what does my being here do to or for them? Beyond the likelihood that my honeybees pollinate some of their garden flowers, I've no notion. As the years tick by, I try to keep my eyes and ears open, try to gauge the nature of this little street's social metabolism, try to detect the ways in which I have and have not yet been assimilated into it.

Then there's the street's other metabolism, its biophysical one, to be attended to. And here, "street" can stand for the world, the planet. Its metabolism operates as an analogue to the organic metabolism of my house, and in turn to that of my own body, for house and body necessarily exist within the world. American property rights law may decree this old arts-and-crafts bungalow to be my castle (so long as the mortgage payments keep flowing), but its sturdy stone walls deceive: they really form a skin, a permeable membrane. Let the autumn weather change abruptly and the air in my house will register the shift, prompting a trip on my part to the thermostat and then to the closet for a sweater. Water, fruits and vegetables of all sorts, some of them grown by people I'll never meet, and bread made by careful hands in a local bakery—these pass through my walls as well, in both directions, on a fairly regular basis. The materials of comfortable, middle-class existence enter the house and sometimes leave again, as sewage or compostables if they're readily biodegradable, as recyclables or trash bound for a landfill if they're not. My dog comes in through that brown front door, as does the occasional visiting friend, as of course do I, all of us bringing along something of the street's effluent, whatever that might include. Now and then a moth, fly, cricket, grasshopper, or mouse traipses through, too, along with trillions of creatures—mites, midges, and microbes—that one (thankfully) never lays eyes upon. Taking direction from the wise, caring people who have been my teachers over the years, I've made a pact with these and all the critters that dwell beyond my front and back steps—the snakes slipping away into small holes in the yard, the mockingbirds and starlings filling the trees, the cicadas flitting and buzzing among the leaves, the thousands of earthworms worming their way up, down, around, and clean through this patch of earth that is currently mine to tend. The pact I've made amounts to a silent agreement with my two-footed neighbors as well, both those I know and those I never will. Simply put, I try not to poison any of them, or to support with my money activities under way in the world that would poison them or their kin. Probably the one aspect of daily life in which I manage this reasonably well is obtaining food, as I either grow my own or try to buy organic whenever possible. But by no means is my promise an easy one to keep in every instance; to cite just one out of many, sometimes I do need to drive, in spite of the noxious gases coming from the tailpipe, or the more-than-noxious mechanisms that brought fuel to my local service station in the first place. Nevertheless, making the effort to stick to my pact whenever possible does approach, I hope, a kind of disciplined living. To be disciplined is to be tutored, shaped, and readied—if I understand the concept aright—for the arrival of wisdom. Not yet old, I nevertheless aspire to wise-woman status.

All three metabolisms, then—of my own life, of my home, of the world beyond my home—need to come into close alignment with one another, such that the tumblers fall into place just so, and a lock clicks open, and a door swings wide: upon what, I'm not sure, but I suspect it's glorious. Wendell Berry points out the shared etymologies of words like "whole" and "holy," reminding us that fragmentation—the imperfectly fitted metabolisms, say, of the various components of daily life—amounts to a form of violence, a violation of something that might otherwise be sacred. Somehow that idea sounds so right to me as to suggest a reason to live, and to try living in a certain way.

In ordinary discourse, and especially in American politics, ecological and economic interests are often thought to be—indeed, are often contrived to appear—antithetical to each other. A most unfortunate development, in an age when we should know better, for the very words share a syllable that must be key to all that any of us really holds dear: "eco" is Greek for "home." Whereas "ecology" denotes the study of the home, "economy" is Greek for management of the home—this earthly home, we might easily imagine the two terms to suggest. My long years of professional study, training, and practice lie in neither field, yet increasingly I sense that the real work I have before me in the coming seasons will involve both. No other work seems nearly so vital; none other seems nearly so scary, so difficult, so exciting, or so sure to require every last ounce of my own modest powers. A body could do worse, I tell myself by way of summoning courage, than put these to their fullest use before moving on to some other, as yet unknown address.

7

Sweetness and Light

We are surrounded by a rich and fertile mystery. May we not probe it, pry into it, employ ourselves about it, a little? To devote your life to the discovery of the divinity in nature or to the eating of oysters, would they not be attended with very different results?

—HENRY DAVID THOREAU,
Journal, September 7, 1851

I.

Seventeen years we've been together, and he has yet to speak to me. Seventeen years, and not one word of kindness, encouragement, solace, inquiry, complaint, not even a simple word of greeting. Ain't that just like a man, I tease him, taking his pointy snout and velvety nose into my hands, gently boxing his ears. Dark, kohl-rimmed eyes search mine quizzically for a fleeting moment; then he gives his head a vigorous shake and snorts, as if he must break the spell, as if he finds all this attention too pleasant to bear standing still. Starting at the honey-gold fur between his eyes, I smooth it with one finger, moving upward and over the fine bones of his skull. A deep brown widow's peak disappears into the black and brown hair atop his head and between his ears, behind which the fibers lengthen and grow more thickly together, fluffing beneath my hand the farther back toward his neck and shoulders I go. His knobby spine serves as a continental divide for the countless long, coarse hairs cascading down his sides, gold and amber, copper and bronze, all of them dipped generously in dark chocolate at the ends; patches of white on his belly show only when he rolls over on his back, which rarely happens now. Until the white began to creep up between his forelegs and into his geriatric jowls and chin, my dog—a Chow and Border Collie mix—was roughly the color of a honeybee, minus the stripes.

In the first year after I rescued him in his puppyhood from the pound, the wildest notion occasionally gripped me: Ben-dog was about to speak! I'd be doing something mindless like raising a window shade, hardly aware he had followed me into the room, when suddenly I would turn to see this little breadbox-size (at the time) creature staring up at me, looking for all the world as if language was on the verge of leaving his half-open, *smiling* mouth, where a big rosy tongue lay quivering in the trough formed by his lower jaw. "What, what?" I'd say out loud to him, dropping to my knees. He'd plow gleefully into my lap for some hugging and wrestling, maybe even knock me back over on my heels laughing, and the moment was gone: the urge to speak had fled him utterly. Once again, I was left to get by strictly on my best understanding of Dog—his whimpering when something hurt, or barking when someone came to the door. Or perhaps (most eloquent of all) his standing quietly forlorn next to an empty food bowl.

Call me a little nuts, maybe, or accuse me of an overactive imagination if you like; I don't mind—indeed, I might respond that imagination is precisely the point. Only by efforts of the imagination will I come the slightest bit close to satisfying a keen desire to connect somehow with this strange and wonderful little being, this four-footer whose rather different physical orientation to the world, and different powers of perception—especially those packed into his remarkable nose—must yield experiences and forms of comprehension that I can, at present, barely guess at. In our respective bodies, my dog and I move through the world as something like open circuits, to borrow a metaphor from the phenomenologist David Abram, circuits that are completed "only in things, in others, in the encompassing earth." That we're not wired to do it—to engage the world, as well as each other—in quite the same way is also why we can't talk with each other about it. We may both communicate through sounds produced in the throat, but that's pretty much where the similarities in our languages begin and end. Ben can't tell me what dogginess is, as lived experience, nor can I get across to him what it's like to live in my furless skin, assuming he'd care to know. And so we remain, ultimately, mysteries to each other.

But not strangers: while I lie on the sofa reading, he sidles up to me and nuzzles my free hand as if to say, *Hey.* Or something like that.

The early-twentieth-century ethnologist Knud Ras-
mussen (according to Abram) recorded this claim of an
Inuit woman he knew:

> In the very earliest time
> when both people and animals lived on earth,
> a person could become an animal if he wanted to
> and an animal could become a human being.
> Sometimes they were people
> and sometimes animals
> and there was no difference.
> All spoke the same language.
> That was the time when words were like magic. . . .

Similar stories abound among indigenous peoples the
globe over: once upon a fabulous and fabled time, they insist, *all creatures could communicate with one another.* We
were all Doctors Doolittle, gabbing happily (for some reason I picture it as a happy period) not just with the wild ancestors of dogs and cats but also with monkeys, elephants,
birds, turtles, toads, even mosquitoes and all the rest, nat-
tering on about everything under the glorious sun, leaving
a great deal less to guesswork than is necessarily now the
case. Now we move through the world in partial exile from
it, whereas in that long-ago time, maybe even plants had
something to say—and we could know their meaning, and
we thought it mattered. Of course, those who believe such
an era ever existed may just be dreaming wistfully, as I
once hoped for the king's English to erupt from Ben. But
still. What I wouldn't give for real access to the myriad

ways these fellow creatures of ours know their lives, know the warm earth squishing between the pads of their paws or cradling their roots, know the air whistling through their leaves or the shafts of their feathers. Could I have it somehow—that access; could the animals and trees tell me their stories, supposing they *would* tell, then surely all of creation must open up for me like a flower, like Christmas all the livelong day.

Tall windows framing old, wavy glass go slowly cobalt as a January evening surrenders to night. From the warm vantage point of my thirties-era Arkansas kitchen, I peer into the shadows pooling about the backyard and see no sign of life near the beehives—more a deep lilac color than their usual white in the fading light—and am not surprised. It's too cold. All I can do is imagine the bees balled up inside, close upon one another and their precious queen, husbanding carefully the embers of life. But just a couple of days ago, before this arctic high-pressure system spilled southward, the temperature was a balmy sixty degrees at midday, so the traffic in front of each hive became almost rush-hour heavy. Once abroad, what drew a bee at this time of year, I wondered, to any given stalk of dead wildflower, or bare branch of dormant shrub? When she scuttled back inside to escape the late-afternoon chill, how did she make her way around in that darkness, and how did the cold-stiffened honeycomb feel beneath her furred feet; what did she make of the apartment's smell, or the crowding jostle of thousands of sister bees?

In short, what's the sum of a honeybee's sensory experience on a winter's day, or for that matter, any day at all?

Because they aren't telling, we must turn to science for some answers if we would begin to fathom how a honeybee knows its life as a bee, knows the world by bee-ing. We might begin with the eyes, naturally enough: as big as they are in proportion to the rest of the honeybee's body, they must be crucial. And they are. But before we get to those two huge eyes, how's this for a well-kept secret: a bee actually has three *additional* eyes, tiny ones clustered at the top of the head and hidden from the casual observer beneath body hair. These ocelli, as they're called, seem designed strictly to gauge light intensity, and not much else. Since they are relatively unimportant, I don't usually go around letting on that they even exist; just about any insect is hard enough to win two-footers over to, without spreading the creepy news that some have an obscenely generous supply of eyes.

Unlike our own, a bee's compound eyes occur on the sides of its head rather than in front, and although they are huge in relation to the bee's overall size, they are nevertheless small as eyes in the animal world go, so the field of vision available to a bee does not extend more than a few feet ahead and to the sides. Also very much unlike our own, each eye is composed of several thousand facets—more in the drone's eye than in a worker's or a queen's, because he's got the greater need for clear vision, if he would find true love and reproduce successfully. (Each facet, interestingly, takes the same hexagonal shape as a cell of

honeycomb. Is it just me, or is this one heck of a coinci-
dence?) The eye even sports lashes, though not the kind
with which we're familiar: whereas a protective fringe
graces the edge of a human eyelid, these teensy honeybee
hairs show up all across the insect's eyeball, wherever those
facets join one another; evidently they help the bee to
gauge wind speed and direction, important to a creature
who must memorize accurately the flight path between her
hive and a food source to which she and her sisters will
want to return.

Those thousands of facets, now, they warrant further
examination all by themselves. A cross-sectional diagram
of one compound eye suggests a lady's broad, open fan,
with each slender slat of the fan representing one of the
facets. The wide end, open to the world, bears a lens at its
tip for collecting light. Just below (in the diagram; behind,
in the actual eye) the lens is an inverted, pigmented cone
that concentrates and focuses light, and below that—
reaching deep into the back of the eye—is a long shaft full
of retinal cells for perceiving light and sending images to
the brain. In cross section these shafts appear to come close
together at the base of the "fan," connecting at that point
to strands of tissue, all bearing nerve cells. Nine types of receptor cells have been identified, variously functioning to
recognize green, blue, ultraviolet, and polarized light—the
latter two of which, we humans can't usually perceive. Of
polarized light we have had occasion to speak: these are
the rays of sun a bee uses to mark its location in the sky despite cloudy or overcast weather. The honeybee's ability to
detect ultraviolet light is yet another important tool in her

survival kit, for this is the light which reveals, in flowers customarily visited by honeybees, a dark spot in the center and accompanying lines extending out to the edges of the petals, like so many spokes from the hub of a wheel. Invisible to us in most cases, these nectar guides make foraging a no-brainer for just about any bee landing along the blossom's outer rim.

Put all of her receptor cells for sight into action at once, and what does a honeybee's brain decide? That the world is very much a mosaic of color, mostly violets, blues, greens, and (to a lesser extent) yellows and oranges—never reds, which a bee sees as shades of gray—and that its forms are never more clearly visible than when they're in motion. Whereas a human eye presents a high-resolution image, a honeybee eye does not, so long as the thing observed remains perfectly still. But let it twitch or sway or tremble, run, jump, or skip, and that wary little bee will have its number. Not that she'll always give a hoot, or a buzz. If you aren't a blooming flower, or a drop of honey, and if you aren't threatening the colony in some way, she won't care—won't even know, in any sense that we'd recognize—whether you live or die.

Surely this sharper vision for whatever's moving accounts for the advice most beekeepers readily impart to the novice: if, while you're working with a hive, the bees grow agitated and come at you threateningly, drop your hands to your sides and stand motionless. They won't easily see you right there before them, large as life, while you're doing your very best tree imitation. But this stratagem is less than foolproof. They may indeed come at you if they smell danger. Which is often the case, simply because you're sweating like nobody's business.

Smell they accomplish with two long, blacker-than-black antennae, each made up primarily of a flagellum segmented into ten parts. All along its length lie thousands of microscopic sensory structures falling into seven types: some are open pits, some are "pore plates" (tiny plates bearing rows of minuscule pores, through which odor-bearing molecules pass), and some are one or another type of hair. Besides telling a bee what the world smells like—most importantly, telling her when and where something smells sweet—the antennae are thought to tell her as well how humid the ambient air is, how warm or cold it is, and even what something tastes like. (Her feet also help in the taste department: imagine stepping onto your kitchen floor and knowing right away that that grit under your soles came from someone using the saltshaker none too tidily.) Further, each antenna bears in two different places an "ear"—a thin snippet of membrane sensitive to nearby sounds occurring at vibration rates ranging from twenty to two hundred or three hundred beats per second, some of which we can't pick up, never mind that our ears are so many hundreds of times larger than a bee's. She also has a set of membranes for hearing located on the insides of her legs; these are what detect a queen's piping to other, as yet unborn, queens, causing the worker to freeze momentarily in her tracks, as though awaiting orders from on high.

The worker bee, more than the drone or queen, knows and manipulates her world largely through her mouth. She's got strong mandibles for gripping and chewing things like pollen grains, propolis, and beeswax. She also uses them to move food around in the hive, whether it be honey or royal jelly or brood food (glandular secretions mixed with digestive enzymes, honey, and water), to groom herself, to haul dead bees and other bits of trash out of the hive, and even, when necessary, to fight. An especially important structure in her mouth is the proboscis, essentially a tube surrounding a tongue. She can extend it some five to seven millimeters when it suits her to do so, or fold it up into a Z and tuck it into her mouth when she needs it out of her way. It's this proboscis that's responsible, during most of a worker's life, for lapping up the queen's pheromones and passing them on to the rest of the colony. At the foraging stage, the worker uses her proboscis to gather groceries—the nectar and water she goes in search of each day around the neighborhood—and to suck up for herself, or give out to another bee (as the situation may require), honey. To take something in, she pumps it up a slender channel running the length of her proboscis and into her mouth, whence it enters the esophagus. From there it goes down into her stomach or crop, which serves much of the time as an expandable internal rucksack for transporting liquids. Now and then the bee herself needs a little nutriment, of course, so nature has provided her with a valve in the back of her crop through which a small portion of her loot—including the occasional morsel of pollen—can move into her midgut for immediate digestion. What she hasn't used for herself gets regurgitated later within the hive, and duly handled by the house bees.

When nest building or repair is under way, the worker's

jaws get some help in manipulating wax and propolis from tiny claws found at the tips of her six legs. Each of her two front legs also includes an antenna cleaner: a brushy notch located right where two leg segments join, with an accompanying spur. To keep her antennae dust-free and sending clear signals to the brain, a bee periodically pulls them, one at a time, through these notches, much as an auto mechanic pulls the oil dipstick of a car through one fist wrapped in a cleaning rag. The bee's two middle legs are her simplest, serving essentially as helpmates to the other legs whenever she wants to walk, or grip a surface, or move solid materials from the front of her body toward her two back legs.

These last a honeybee worker could not do without and still remain the least bit respectable—that is, useful—among her sisters. Each hind leg's most important structure is the corbicula, a concave depression located in the middle segment and furnished with hair at the edges as well as a single, stiff hair in the center. This one bristle acts as a hook or anchor for a balled-up load of cargo: pollen or propolis that has been collected by mandibles and front legs, moistened with a little regurgitated honey, and pressed into the corbicula by rubbing action from the opposite hind leg, in combination with vigorous pumping by the original leg. Next time you see a honeybee lift off a flower and head hiveward, watch closely: those hind legs aren't rubbing each other out of simple satisfaction, the way you might rub your hands together to express pleasure over a job well done. Those legs are going at it because the job *isn't* yet done: unless and until she gets the goods safely back home, the bee's foraging efforts have been for naught.

So she uses her flying time constructively, maneuvering her freight carefully about her person so as not to drop any.

As she flies, then, we can be fairly sure our honeybee feels the wind caress all her hairy little self, that she sees the earth rushing away beneath her, and that she registers the air temperature and its relative humidity. She detects as well the current strength of the earth's magnetic field, which varies slightly over the course of a day. This she does by means of thousands, perhaps millions, of magnetite crystals or "lodestones" located in abdominal cells known as trophocytes. Other animals in need of navigational equipment (think salmon, think homing pigeons) make use of similar crystals. Although the precise use to which a bee puts them while wandering the planet remains incompletely understood, it stands to reason this sensitivity to magnetism augments nicely all her other sensory devices.

A bee's wings are actually extensions of the skeleton, which, in any insect, takes the place of skin. Imagine, if you will, the shoulder blades across your back growing very, very thin, at the same time that they break through your skin and spread themselves out to the point of translucence. The bee actually sports not one but two pairs of these remarkable accessories, all four of them sprouting from the rear portion of her thorax. The smaller pair—the hind wings—might give a bee in flight more headache than help, were it not for the fact that she can latch them onto the bottom edge of the larger pair with a short row of tiny hooks to streamline her profile and reduce resistance while she's airborne. And those veins across the wing surface, so suggestive of pane divisions in a stained-glass window?

Conduits for blood, air, and nerves, doubling as struts for enhanced wing strength. Sometimes you'll hear it said that a honeybee's physique makes flight anatomically impossible, especially the really fast flight (two hundred cycles of the wings per second, would you believe, for an average airspeed of twenty-four kilometers, or fifteen miles, per hour) that she does in fact exhibit. What such claims don't take into account, however, is that a bee isn't built like other winged insects, who power themselves along with muscles directly connected to their appendages, like so many bugs strung up between kites. No, the honeybee's body has dispensed with such inefficiency and come to rely instead on the alternating action of vertical and longitudinal muscles in the thorax: a rapid series of up-down, side-to-side contractions and relaxations of that segment of her back to which the wings are fastened. Were we to catch this on camera and slow it down, the bee would seem to be vibrating as she zooms along. Small wonder, then, that this little powerhouse is producing excess heat, which moves through her blood to her head, where it finds release in regurgitated droplets of water-diluted honey; these in turn serve to cool her harried brow.

That's right, you heard it here first: a honeybee sweats honey, the very fuel that has sustained all that zipping around the neighborhood. Much as you or I, living on an exclusive diet of beets or garlic, would probably sweat beet or garlic juice.

A honeybee that's just come upon a promising nectar source—a field of white clover launching into bloom, let's say—quickly becomes one excited little bug. "Gold!" we might imagine her buzzing to herself. She makes a beeline for the hive, eager to spread the good news. Once there, she flits around inside to attract attention, then leads several dozen sisters out of the hive and straight back to the clover, right? After all, she's the one who knows where it is, and it could be as much as a mile or two from home, over hill and crazy dale, so if she's going to have help tapping all that sweetness, she's got to lead her team of assistants to the goods.

Sounds reasonable, but for one hitch: it isn't true. Centuries of beekeepers and bee-watchers thought it happened that way, so we might be forgiven if we assumed as much, too. However, at the start of the twentieth century, Maurice Maeterlinck, one of a long line of scribbling beekeepers, discovered otherwise, according to the science writers James and Carol Gould. Having captured a foraging bee and marked her with a bit of paint, Maeterlinck set her free to resume foraging. Back at the hive, he lay in wait for her, let her enter, then recaptured her before she could depart the hive once more. Then he hurried to the food source: sure enough, bees began arriving—yet they hadn't followed the messenger, because she hadn't been free to lead them there.

They had gotten there by way of a map she'd given them, a mental map. A map she had roughly sketched out for her compatriots while inside the hive on the face of a piece of honeycomb, using her whole body as a kind of stylus.

"No competent scientist *ought* to believe these things!"

Karl von Frisch is reported to have exclaimed. But he it was who broke the code—who learned how to understand Honeybee, rather as you or I might understand Dog—so he had to believe, almost in spite of himself. Switching metaphors, so as to speak of this mapmaking in common parlance, we would say that the honeybee who discovers botanical gold communicates knowledge of her find not with a drawing but with a dance—one of two that she has in her repertoire. If she wants to indicate to her sisters (a dozen or more will stop what they're doing to watch a returning forager) that the food source is relatively close by, she does what's called the round dance: she moves in quick, tight circles, clockwise first, then counterclockwise, et cetera, several times, tracing a figure eight. The speed and degree of energy she gives to her dance suggests to the others the relative wealth of the nectar or pollen source. Is she just sort of moseying along? Not much out there, then, so only a few bees will be dispatched to go collect it. Is she twirling like a teenager whose all-time major love-crush just asked her to the prom? Then greater numbers of recruits will race off in search of the implied booty.

If the food source is some distance away, our forager skips the round dance in favor of her other routine, the "waggle dance." This entails repeatedly waggling her abdomen sideways while running in one direction a few paces, circling to the right till she reaches her starting point, again running the straight line and waggling, then circling to the left for the return to her original position, and so forth. But how do the bees glean from this dance a sense of the distance to be covered to reach the food—that is, how far away from the hive is "far"? Through numerous experiments, Von Frisch determined that incrementally greater distances resulted in slower dance tempos and increased numbers of wags. He even demonstrated variations in these factors from one variety of honeybee to another—dialects, essentially, in the dance language. A graph of these variations shows (for example) that *A. m. ligustica*'s dance includes more wags per one hundred meters of distance from hive to food source than does *A. m. carnica*'s, but not as many as that of *A. m. lamarckii*. In the same way that I might tell you Little Rock lies about twenty minutes' drive from my home, a bee conveys distance to her sisters in terms of how long they must fly to reach dinner, but among the races, slightly different terms, or waggle rates, are used to refer to the same distance.

Still with me? All right, then. Picture yourself as one of those sister honeybees watching the dance. You're thrilled to know there's clover out there (the scent clinging to the dancer gives you that important tidbit, so you'll know what to sniff the air for as you get close) and the pace of her dancing tells you about how far you'll have to fly to hit the jackpot. But you need another clue. From the hive's entrance, in which direction do you take off? The dance conveys that key piece of information, too. If your messenger begins her dance by running straight up the vertical face of the honeycomb, she's telling you the field of flowers lines up with the sun, so from the hive you'll head sunward. If she's running down the comb, she's saying the opposite, that you should fly in a direct line away from the sun. If she runs a few degrees to either the right or left of the vertical, you can bet the field lies at an angle that many degrees to the right or left of the sun.

Von Frisch figured all this out as well, and for his trouble took home a Nobel Prize to hang on his wall.

The Goulds point out that these dance routines are properly considered a "language" because they "[satisfy] all the intuitive criteria that have been posited for a true language." The dances convey not just excitement, but fairly precise information about some part of the world located well away from the hive in time and space. "Moreover," the Goulds add, "the conventions for dance communication are arbitrary: the bees interpret the direction of the sun as 'up'; it could just as easily be 'down' or '20 [degrees] to the left of vertical,' as long as both sender and receiver agree to abide by the convention. In fact, the use of the sun's direction at all is arbitrary; it could just as easily have been the direction the hive faces, or true or magnetic north." Likewise, we English speakers could have chosen to say "cat" when we wanted to refer to a scaled thing that lives full-time underwater, and that would have worked fine so long as everyone speaking English agreed to call it that. Because bees of a given race already know their assigned dialect—their waggle rate, as a measure of distance—upon emergence as adults from their little wax wombs, we would not say the dance language is in any way learned. It is innate, and it is non-transferable across races: pupae of one race placed experimentally in the hive of another will emerge to find themselves unable to communicate accurately with the predominate race and thus will prove worse than useless, handing out bad directions all around, and misunderstanding those handed to them.

Perhaps all this is quite wild enough in itself. But hold on, there's more. A dancing bee is also a singing bee: the Goulds report that a waggling forager "produces a motorboat-like sound by moving her wing muscles (with wings folded) in short bursts about a thirtieth of a second long," apparently to reinforce or reiterate, as it were, what her dance is saying about distance. And *her* song may be met by another: a single, quick note struck by a bee watching the dance—which has the effect of stopping the dancer and compelling her to surrender a dollop of the food whose praises she's been, ah, singing. Tasting it, the recipient now knows beyond a doubt what she'll be searching for when she heads for the hills.

Food shopping may be one of the most crucial subjects of conversation within the hive, but it isn't the only one. Another is the question that must occasionally be entertained of whether to build some new queen cells, perhaps to replace a failing queen or to begin laying the groundwork for a swarm. James and Carol Gould suggest that a "decision" to build or not to build new royal apartments can take days, maybe weeks, to reach, and it is accomplished through conflicting behaviors on the parts of many, many house bees. Some begin adding vertical flakes of wax to the bottom of a frame of comb, while others, happening upon these flakes, rip them partially away; another bee may come along and continue ripping, or commence repairing the earlier damage and adding more wax. "Each bee is casting a vote," say the Goulds, for or against building new cells and raising new queens. Gradually a preponderance of bees does either more building than wrecking or vice versa, until the votes lie wholly on one side of the question. So although honeybees are famous for thinking and behaving as one colony, one "superorganism," it ain't entirely so at all times—and a good thing, too. This capacity for expressing and weighing different views of a problem is, the Goulds explain, "highly adaptive: it allows for faster, more flexible and finely graded control than would be possible if all acted with one mind." Calling this process "a lesson in participatory democracy," these science writers, perhaps unwittingly, join the ranks of countless others who have drawn from the hive a political moral.

II.

The justly famous dances of the honeybees are thought of by some as a form of poetry in motion. And why not? Poetry, too, aims to communicate, and, like the dances, poetry usually wants to send its audience out into the world to see and taste it afresh. Literature generally has served this dual purpose for a very long time. The Roman poet Horace wrote that the aim of literary expression should be "to blend in one [work] the delightful and the useful," that which, in his own words, is *dulce* (sweet) and *utile* (useful). The writer who "mingles the useful with the sweet carries the day by charming his reader and at the same time instructing him." By "useful" instruction Horace meant enlightenment, moral insight, even moral improvement—and he seems to have sensed that such medicine goes down best with a spoonful of sugar.

Now, for all we know, honeybees were the last things on the poet's mind as he penned these thoughts. But hundreds of years later, a prominent Irish man of letters with a particular ax to grind saw a connection.

In the years just before and after the turn of the eighteenth century, a handful of European intellectuals and wits got into a scrappy little argument that they carried on for some time in London's coffeehouses, Paris's cafés, and a variety of published and widely read works. At issue was the question of which kind of learning better served humanity: that embodied by the works of classical Greece and Rome, or that characteristic of contemporary efforts within newly emerging disciplines, wherein the knowledge of classical thinkers was being updated, corrected, and in some cases debunked and discredited, not always for good scholarly reasons. The two debating camps were dubbed, respectively, the Ancients and the Moderns; the former are more commonly remembered now as neoclassicists. In the early Greek and Roman works of metaphysical, political, and natural philosophy, those grand old specimens of poetry and mathematics, astronomy, sculpture, history, architecture, and all the rest—in these things could be found, the neoclassicists believed, much of what one could know of the true, the good, and the beautiful. More important even than what these works said was the frame of mind with which the authors typically approached their subjects: that of the interdisciplinary generalist, whose fundamental belief about the world was that all of its parts are ultimately of a piece, unified. That we live inescapably, as Wendell Berry has said more recently, in a *uni*-verse. (The poet Richard Wilbur asserts that this "unity of all things"—his words—explains the nature of metaphor, which has the unique ability to call attention to underlying likenesses among apparently disparate entities.) Further, the "Ancients" felt, such a belief tends to cultivate in one a becoming modesty, for the self is seen as but a tiny stitch in a vast fabric, the farthest edges of which remain unknown, and very likely unknowable.

In the Moderns, conversely, the neoclassicists saw an alarming, puffed-up self-regard borne of achievements within narrow spheres—achievements that, to the Ancients' way of thinking, did little to heighten the nobility of humankind and even less to improve, morally speaking, the men who were their authors. One favorite target was the textual scholar and editor Richard Bentley, who, in fact, happened to work on classical texts. Called by his detractors Slashing Bentley for the relish with which he emended texts to suit himself, this Modern embodied all that was wrong with his kind: in him technical expertise was divorced from taste, knowledge divorced from virtue. He was too much the specialist, with a brash tendency to remove scholarly questions or problems from their historical and human contexts. Which approach, the Ancients averred, could result only in intellectual mischief: while it might ignore the uni-versality of things, it did not change this basic truth (because nothing could); the upshot could only be, then, the doing of violence to the essential nature of the world, and to the mysterious relationships among its countless parts.

Bentley and his ilk were spiders, accused an anonymous satirist of the neoclassical persuasion, spinning a spurious—even poisonous—knowledge out of their own fevered brains into flimsy webs that lasted, where they lasted for any measurable time at all, only in dusty library nooks unvisited by genuinely curious minds, who knew to look elsewhere for better material.

The satirist proved to be none other than Jonathan Swift; the deliciously wicked mock epic he had published in 1704 to attack the Moderns was called *The Battle of the Books*; and over and against the spider's, or Modern's, shallow, self-referential, pseudo-learning he posited that of the classical writer, represented by—can you guess?—the honeybee. The bee spins no webs out of himself (Swift depicts it as a male) but instead roams creation in search of the best the world has to offer. His greatest attributes are his wings and his voice, for with the one he can take flight in many directions, thus giving free rein to his insatiable curiosity, "ranging through every corner of nature," while with the other he can communicate, in mellifluous, murmuring tones, what he has found. By means of his wide travels and his rich capacity for synthesizing internally all that he has gathered from outside himself, the bee brings humanity "the two noblest of things," things which can soothe, nourish, and banish the dark: honey and wax. In the next breath Swift called them—taking a page from Horace—sweetness and light.

(In his use of the honeybee to suggest intellectual curiosity, Swift may also have had the French essayist Michel de Montaigne in mind, who had similarly praised the bee's eclecticism, seeing in it a parallel to the essayist's art. Or maybe Swift was thinking of the natural philosopher Francis Bacon, who had seen in the bee the perfect scientist—one who takes the best results of both the exercise of reason and the collection of empirical data, and "lays [them] up in the understanding changed and refined," much as a bee selects various nectars and blends them into honey. Just about every intellectual generalist, it seems, eventually gets around to looking in a mirror and seeing *Apis mellifera*.)

In reaching for the honey-and-wax analogy, the sweetness-and-light phrase, Swift knew he could count on many of his contemporary readers—especially his fellow Ancients—to pick up the allusion to Horace's *Ars Poetica* and the message it implied: that the quality of our learning, as we pursue it and as we share it with others in our works, should be measured by the degree to which it ennobles and enriches human life. It is our works, after all, that will help to shape the learning of others—that will help to form and inform their understanding of the world, and the spirit in which they will move through it, use it, care for it, and pass it on.

Some one hundred sixty years after Swift, the poet and literary critic Matthew Arnold resurrected this theme, as well as the Irishman's phrase, when he wrote that the pursuit of culture amounts to "but one great passion, the passion for sweetness and light." The pursuit of culture, for Arnold, was the pursuit of individual spiritual growth—of perfection, he actually claimed, which he equated with the will of God. "Not a having and a resting, but a growing and a becoming, is the character of perfection as culture conceives it," he added, "and here . . . it coincides with religion" and "follows one law with poetry." It is hard not to hear in these words an echo of Keats's idea that truth is beauty, and beauty truth; hard not to glimpse, in this insistence that culture is a thing to be pursued, the image of a young man forever chasing his beloved around the exquisite curve of a Grecian urn. The pursuit of perfection, Arnold went on, entails "increased spiritual activity, having for its characters increased sweetness, increased light, increased life, increased sympathy. . . ."

Arnold's target in this section of *Culture and Anarchy* was the shallow (to him) idea in vogue that culture was little more than a highbrow affectation of learning, and the companion idea that culture could be spread, like some thin veneer, among the populace by means of mass-marketed, popular literature, what we now call pop culture. He was taking aim as well at his contemporaries' infatuation with "machinery," which included financial wealth as well as the literal machines of the Industrial Revolution, among other things. His fellow Englishmen had come to see increased quantities of these, over the course of the nineteenth century, as signs of successful civilization, forgetting that they are really only tools, best used in the service, ultimately, of the individual person's inner improvement. To pursue wealth and technology for their own sake was, for Arnold, to take a serious wrong turn away from the more important path of genuine human growth;

to hand the masses of people that which passed for literature in the popular press was to deprive them of genuine
light, genuine sweetness, and to expect them to make do
with sham substitutes.

Okay, okay, Arnold, Swift, Horace—this is all very well
and good, you say, but haven't we mislaid the honeybees
somewhere along the way here?

Not really, no. I think of these moldy old ghosts when,
as happens fairly often, someone asks me why a body
would bother with keeping beehives when they don't always yield much honey, or when you have to risk a few
stings to get it, or when the stuff is so much more easily
bought across town at Kroger. *For sweetness and light,
that's why. For beauty and truth,* I want to say. But I don't
usually, wimping out instead with a grin and a shrug. I
think of Arnold when the Ben-dog and I step out of the
house each night, him to pee and me to lose myself for a
spell, staring up at the stars, while the windows of houses
all around me glow neon blue with the latest episode of, I
don't know, *Desperate Housewives* or something. A neighbor who has noticed this evening routine and who knows I
work at the university asks me in all seriousness whether I
am an astronomer. He does not believe me right away
when I respond with amused denial; he seems not to believe the stars are for anyone but specialists to take an interest in. He does not know that the night sky belongs to
him the moment he chooses to lay claim to it, that the
swelling moon will light up his life the same as it will that
of any Turkoman or king. He seems not to realize that at

least some of his exile from the world that gave birth to him—the same one that still fuels the beating of his heart—is self-imposed. I think of this man, and then I think of Ralph Waldo Emerson, who wrote that if the stars were to come out just once in the entire history of the world, everyone would fall over themselves getting outside to see. But since they're out night after night after night and again after that, they offer ordinary people little novelty; they become mere backdrop to more important things—such as, I suppose, the blinking red lights of cell phone towers, or the sporty late-model cars cruising down the street.

Some spring mornings, I pull a stool up near one of my hives to wait for the first bee to shake off her lethargy and step outside, eager to begin her day. And I may think then of Annie Dillard, finding what she called pennies from heaven in the furl of a mockingbird's wing, or in the greening of the spring grass. I think of Mary Austin back at the turn of the twentieth century, laying out her bedroll in the Southwest desert sage, next to a campfire, taking notes in its flickering light and falling asleep to the distant keening of wolves. I think of this huge continent of ours, with many pockets of arresting interest and impossible beauty still left to it, and of all the American citizens therein who get around on four legs or six, or no legs at all, the finned ones plying dark waters, the feathered ones bright shafts of air and light; who do not (as Whitman said) whine about their condition, even if we've given them plenty of reason to, with our ill manners, our thoughtlessness, our rapacity. I think of a particular stretch of beach I know well, and of a dusky swamp I used to paddle around in with my old canoe, where a prehistorically strange great blue heron suffered my steady gaze one evening for a solid hour, while it went about its silent spear-fishing. And wonder to myself, what have I seen, why have I seen it, what does it mean.

I think of William James, who once mused that God may reveal himself only to those who want and expect revelation. Those who, as Martin Buber wrote, have heard this stunning world call them by name, and who have paused to cock an ear, straining to catch what will come next.

PARTIAL LIST OF SOURCES

David Abram, *The Spell of the Sensuous: Perception and Language in a More-than-Human World*. New York: Pantheon, 1996.

The American Bee Journal. Various issues since 2002.

Ian G. Barbour, *Religion and Science: Historical and Contemporary Issues*. New York: HarperCollins, 1997.

J. F. Bierlein, *Parallel Myths*. New York: Ballantine, 1994.

Stephen L. Buchmann and Gary Paul Nabhan, *The Forgotten Pollinators*. Washington, D.C.: Island Press, 1996.

Eva Crane, *The World History of Beekeeping and Honey Hunting*. London: Duckworth, 1999.

Dadant & Sons, eds., *The Hive and the Honey Bee*. 1946. Hamilton, Ill.: Dadant & Sons, 1975.

Lee Dugatkin, *Cheating Monkeys and Citizen Bees: The Nature of Cooperation in Animals and Humans*. New York: Free Press, 1999.

Karl von Frisch, *The Dancing Bees: An Account of the Life*

and Senses of the Honey Bee. Trans. Dora Ilse. New York: Harcourt, 1953.

James L. Gould and Carol Grant Gould, *The Honey Bee.* New York: Scientific American Library, 1988; 1995.

Leon Kass, *The Hungry Soul: Eating and the Perfecting of Our Nature.* 1994. University of Chicago Press, 1999.

Rebecca Solnit, *A Field Guide to Getting Lost.* New York: Viking, 2005.

Douglas Whynott, *Following the Bloom: Across America with the Migratory Beekeepers.* 1991. New York: Penguin, 2004.

Mark L. Winston, *The Biology of the Honey Bee.* Cambridge, Mass: Harvard UP, 1987.

About the Author

ALLISON WALLACE has published many articles and essays. She is a professor of American Studies at the Honors College of the University of Central Arkansas. She lives in Conway, Arkansas, and *A Keeper of Bees* is her first book.

About the Type

This book was set in Sabon, a typeface designed by the well-known German typographer Jan Tschichold (1902–74). Sabon's design is based upon the original letter forms of Claude Garamond and was created specifically to be used for three sources: foundry type for hand composition, Linotype, and Monotype. Tschichold named his typeface for the famous Frankfurt typefounder Jacques Sabon, who died in 1580.